THE HUNTING
OF THE SHARK

to Mark + Helen.
It's good to know
you are sharkists.
all best Wishes.
Bill Heine
10 April 12

DEDICATION

To Sculptor John Buckley, who made the Shark

THE HUNTING OF THE SHARK

BILL HEINE

An OXFORDFOLIO Book
© Bill Heine, 2011

46 Hayfield Road, Oxford, 0X2 6TU
www.oxfordfolio.co.uk

Editor: **James Harrison**
Designer: **Nick Withers**

Printed by Butler Tanner & Dennis, Frome, UK

ISBN: 978-0-9567405-2-6

British Library Cataloguing-in-Publication Data

A catalogue record for this book is available from the British Library

10 9 8 7 6 5 4 3 2 1

Some think its good
Some think its bad
Some think its funny
And that the owner is mad

From
Matthew
Curtis age 8

" *I could have said 'No. Stop, I can't take the pain'; but in that attic I am able to deal with the damage because I don't know how extensive it will be. I have no idea the battle to keep the shark crashing through the shattered tiles of my roof in Oxford will rage for six years through the council, the courts and even the Cabinet. I don't know about the political knives, the dirty tricks and the naked hatred. I am unaware of walking into a particularly English minefield reserved for 'the rebel.'* "

PART ONE

A SHARK ATTACK IN
LACE CURTAIN LAND

DATELINE: 8ᵀᴴ AUGUST, 1986

Sculptor John Buckley shaves the styrofoam model of the Shark at his chicken farm studio and creates a 'summer snow fall' on the ground.

1

The shark will arrive early tomorrow morning. I am waiting for the reception committee – two off-duty fire-fighters who are going to smash open my roof and allow the shark to slip in. We don't want to give the game away to my neighbours so we leave the hatchet job on the roof as late in the day as possible. No need to advertise and upset people unnecessarily early. This is the first step; it has to be done discreetly.

I don't usually stand by my front door – at No. 2 New High Street, Headington, Oxford – wearing Doc Martins and combat trousers, stripped to the waist with a surgical mask hanging around my neck and a pickaxe in my hand at tea-time like a latter day Tom Sawyer. Perhaps that's what attracts someone to open my gate and accost me, an Oxford version of Tom Sawyer's Aunt Polly, a pillar of the New High Street Residents Association.

After a few pleasantries June Whitehouse, who looks like she has eaten every pleasantry on the menu a few times, comes to the point. 'Bill, I've heard . . . now forgive me because this is going to sound a bit off the wall . . . but I've heard that you plan to put a shark in your roof. Is this true?' Her voice is high and not quite cracking. She is in earnest. I am incensed. I'm also somewhat taken aback, not only by the directness of her question but also by the fact that the news has leaked out. So my sense of shock is real enough. 'June, why would I do that? Why would anyone? Wouldn't that be insane? Where did you hear such a story?'

She isn't convinced. 'Well a journalist from the *Oxford Courier* has been walking up and down the street, knocking on everyone's door asking our reaction. I did question him about what he meant, and I'll admit he was a bit flaky; so I wanted to check with you.' Damn the *Oxford Courier*. They were the only newspaper I left off my list. Now they were obviously out for revenge, and they could have scuppered it. If anyone had taken them seriously I might be talking to a court bailiff with an injunction instead of my neighbour with a floral dress.

I turn the pickaxe upside down to sit on it and get the thing out of her sight line. 'Look, June, this is a quiet, residential area of Oxford with leafy lanes, lace curtains and people like you and me where neighbours don't do things like that, do they? This is a perfectly fine roof; why would I want to rip it apart?' That does the trick. 'Well, exactly! I'm glad to hear it,' she responds, 'I'm sure everyone will be so relieved.'

I haven't quite lied. Well let's be honest . . . I haven't lied at all, just asked a few questions, the kind that I couldn't answer completely myself. June leaves with perfect timing. Two minutes later the fire-fighters arrive incognito. They have hard hats and hacksaws in a holdall. The three of us crawl through a small hole into my attic, an 1850s terraced house attic where nothing much has happened in all that time. Cobwebs, chunks of mortise and the debris of improvements over the years tell the tale. It has been an ordinary attic . . . until now.

The attic space is cramped and sweltering on this August afternoon. The dust has been baked and is hot to the touch. My fire-fighters put on their helmets and take off their shirts. Tom and Dick are in their twenties, fit and up for the adventure. But why do they want to go on this particular journey? As firemen, their aim is to save buildings. Here we are risking the destruction of one. It's like asking a Samaritan to help with an assisted suicide. It doesn't make sense.

And tomorrow the wood work to build a landing pad for the Shark would be done by two people who normally make harpsichords and conservatories. The steel grid to secure the sculpture would be the work of an Irish publican. School teachers, lawyers, labourers and the odd Bavarian Count will all be on hand to make sure it goes smoothly. How insane does it get? How could a cottage industry of amateurs make this Shark fly? When I asked June if it would be insane to put a Shark in my roof, I hit the proverbial nail on the head. Why didn't I just say 'no'?

What am I doing in this version of Dante's *Inferno* where the hottest seat in the hottest circle of hell is reserved for those who in times of decision sit on the fence? I slide off and go back to the two fire-fighters. We survey the inside of the roof. They have directions and put an 'X' – several actually – on the roof felt so they will know where to start hacking. 'Are you ready?' they ask me.

This is it: the moment when you take the one thing we all need, a roof over your head, and you smash it. I can smell the power of these guys; they are ready to begin, itching to start . . . everything we had planned for the last four months is hanging in the balance here. These two fire-fighters just want to check whether it's alright to smash my roof. At this moment I understand for the first time exactly what is going on. It's easy to talk tactics over a tequila; you see things differently in the cockpit. This is, to be blunt, self harm. It's as if I am taking a razor blade to my own skin and I'm about to slash it. I will never be able to undo that.

The silence is sweaty. I break it: 'Yes!' The fire-fighters wield the axe with a grunt, a thud, a crackling of things and a scream – mine. I don't know at the time if it is pleasure or pain. Lathe and plaster come crashing around us, hissing, stinging and hurting. It is almost as though the roof were fighting back, outraged at the assault.

We are trapped in this hellhole and even with our face masks we choke on the chaos we have created. We need to get this over with to reach the tiles and break out

Looking more like a surfer 'shooting the tube' inside a wave, sculptor John Buckley smoothes and shapes the shark's innards.

'Untitled, 1986" by John Buckley
Mixed Media: fibreglass, bricks, mortar, flowers, curtains, people...

to let some air in. Before they can touch the slates, the fire-fighters have to cut the beams (these solid pieces of strength that are really the bones of the building). It's one thing to slash your skin. It's quite another to break your own arm. A lot of things will break along the way. There will be a great deal of pain and damage because 'the rebel' believes, doesn't know where to stop and will risk everything.

The original invitation to the media for the landing of the shark. The *London Evening Standard* prints a reply in their 'Londoner's Diary':
'Strange invitations have reached me before but none, until this morning [August 7, 1986] , ever began: "I'm writing to ask if you would be interested in a story about a shark crashing into a house." The writer is one William Heine from Oxford. He has, it seems, commissioned a seven metre long fibreglass shark from sculptor John Buckley for the express purpose of dropping it through the roof of his own house on Saturday. "On 9th August," he clarifies, "the roof will be ripped by a thirteen foot hole with tiles falling down and battens sticking up and will look something like the enclosed sketch." The enclosed sketch [*see opposite*] is indeed just as he has described it. It's been captioned: "Mixed Media: fibreglass, bricks, mortar, flowers, curtains, people . . ." William Heine reminds me that Saturday is the anniversary of the bombing of Nagasaki. I cannot believe this is happening.'

'How could a cottage industry of amateurs
make this Shark fly?'

My dreams are pretty risky too – the night is full of planes blowing up, houses crashing down or my neighbours devouring me whole in a bloody ritual of hate, impotence and fear; and I wake up from one nightmare and walk straight into another. Outside my house on a sleepy Saturday morn, a 60-foot crane waddles up the street like a bloated body builder on steroids, followed closely by an even bigger one. I open the front door to a gaggle of reporters and photographers snapping and snooping – demanding to know when the Shark will arrive.

2

SLOUCHING TOWARDS BETHLEHEM

The press are expected. I invited them by sending out drawings of the finished Shark attack by co-conspirator, sculptor John Buckley. They bite big time. But what do you do with visitors at six o'clock in the morning? I make the reporters some tea and hand out a detailed schedule prepared in advance.

This is around the time when Prince Andrew and Fergie tied the knot. The media were used to getting a military-style list of what things would happen when. They wanted to know how the Shark would arrive for the ceremony and the length of time it would take to reach the altar in the roof. Who was going to join the house and the Shark together in this unholy union, and when could they open the Champagne for a toast so they would be able to get the story to their editors in time for the Sunday front pages?

Of course I have no answers to these questions so I simply make it all up. The shark arrives at 7:30 in the morning. with a full escort. By 8:45 the shark is attached to the first crane. The lift from street to the top of the house takes 35 minutes; at 9:20 it is hovering over the hole in the roof until 10:45 when the installation is complete. At 10:50 the second crane hoists a technician to un-harness the tail from the first crane. By 11:00 exactly the sculpture is free-standing and ready for close-ups so the photographers can meet their editors' deadlines of twelve noon.

I thought there might be a few amendments, like the arrival of the police, the storming of the house by my neighbours, and the production of a court order by the bailiffs, but I wanted a tight and tidy schedule and so I omitted these frills. The reporters seem satisfied and settle down to wait for the arrival of the Shark . . .

On a chicken farm twenty miles away in the Thames-side town of Wallingford, Barney Hannaghan turns up to drive a tractor on a mystery tour. The farm hand knows the twelve-foot hayrick is loaded with a twenty-five-foot-long fibreglass Shark, neatly trussed up the night before; but he doesn't know where he is taking it.

Chaos and mayhem around the fibreglass creation as the finishing touches are added.

John Buckley has been creating this piece of art for four months in his studio, a converted chicken shed, and keeps the destination of the Shark secret on a 'strictly need-to-know' basis. When Barney starts the engine he doesn't have a clue. John whispers, 'Take the back roads to Oxford, go to Headington and dodge the police.' It is still night. The tractor doesn't have headlights and the hayrick has no rear lights, so under cover of darkness the Shark nips out from the chicken farm onto the Oxford Road.

The start of the journey is all down hill, but a roundabout is waiting at the bottom junction with a main road between Oxford and Reading. Barney takes the curve slowly. The hayrick tilts precariously. There is a small movement and some tension on the ropes, but the Shark doesn't fall off. Barney takes a swig of black coffee from his thermos. The young man and the Shark are on their way.

So are the reporters. About fifty are milling around in the centre of the street . . . and they keep coming. Word has leaked to the foreign press and Reuters has sent a photographer. When the tea, coffee and juice run out by 7:00 a.m. I realise this Shark story could swim beyond the shores of England.

The installation crews begin to appear. Mark and Antoine, the carpenters, are arguing about how to build the plinth up on the roof. Paddy O'Connor from the Bat & Ball pub in the Oxfordshire village of Cuddesdon arrives with his barman carrying six steel girders and a blow torch. There is a small hiccup – they can't find an extension lead. Sophie, the Polish stage designer, brings the window boxes with red geraniums and blue lobelia, starts hanging the lace curtains and props a papier-mâché head that looks like a Modigliani sculpture on a stick to peer out of the corner of the curtains at the crowd. The artist Catherine Brighton rolls up with the house name plaque she's painted on a wooden shingle – *Untitled, 1986* – and hammers it into place beside the front door.

There are actually quite a few people in on the conspiracy and each one attends to a particular task – like a medical team preparing a patient for the big operation. Not everyone is helpful though. Maybe it is the hubbub of the reporters or the engines of the cranes, but something has woken up this street. Several of my neighbours, some in pyjamas and slippers, others wrapped in robes, wander the pavement like ants whose nest has been disturbed, and these ants are in an ugly mood with big frowns and angry eyes. A few gather behind my back but purposefully near enough so I can hear them: 'This is preposterous! He'll never get away with it!' 'There must be a law against this.' 'We've got to stop him, if he succeeds here what will he do next?' 'I've already called the council. They'll stuff his guns.' 'Well, somebody ought to stuff him!'

There are pockets of displeasure. The mood is getting a bit raw. People don't want to look me in the eye any more. It's as though they are going to a hanging and don't want to confront the condemned man. I move quietly away to welcome new arrivals. The crowd must be up to two hundred now. Things are heating up fast.

Barney is slowly chugging away though the Oxfordshire countryside in his solitary tractor. The sun is up, shining like a spotlight on the Shark: and now that his deed is fully exposed he wonders if there is a law against this Shark lark. He gives the engine a bit of welly and goes hell for leather, but it is a tractor, and in his cab Barney slouches toward this particular Bethlehem at seventeen and a half miles per hour . . . max. He heads down the rural lanes and by-ways to Warborough, negotiates a sharp, tricky turn on a blind bend into Newington and follows the River Thame to Stadhampton. A few early-morning cyclists on their way to work do double takes. One falls off. None of the car drivers seems in a hurry to pass. They are quite content to slow down for a Shark.

Familiar landmarks float past. Wittenham Clumps, site of a Bronze Age fortress, disappears on the horizon; and the spires of Oxford – Tom Tower at Christ Church and the Radcliffe Camera – come into view. Barney is getting closer now and enjoying the bird song and the peaceful isolation.

The crowd must be close to three hundred. Some invisible message has gone out. People are flocking to find out what the lie of the land is: will a Shark crash into the roof of that house or not? Ripples of nervous laughter break out from one group in anticipation of the unexpected. Another group is furious. There is real, deep-seated anger . . . and fear. It bubbles over into shouts. 'This is out of control right here under our noses in our own neighbourhood. Nobody asked us! We're being invaded. Stop it.'

The pillar of the New High Street Residents Association has changed from her robe and is back, but not with a vengeance. She takes the view that the neighbours should wait and see. How do they know this will be blot on the landscape? But it seems that the angry and the eager are about to come to blows. It is a street of swirling emotions. I don't walk away because this is my fight; I watch, shocked by the power of the raw nerves on display. Nothing has happened yet and still some people are ready to hit out when no one really knows if this will work or if we will have a huge mistake on our hands. It's all a big question mark.

One man with an answer is lurking at the edge of the crowd with his camera. He is certain this is all wrong. He keeps taking shots of every movement, every detail. I recognise him; he works for Oxford City Council. But he is only a passing cloud in what is becoming a clear sky. The gossip on the street is growing in favour of the odds that a Shark will arrive. The mood is changing from an atmosphere of people going to a hanging towards something more like people going to a happening. However one hard-bitten Australian journo isn't convinced. He comes up to me pointing at his watch, 'Look mate, it's 6:25. Did you call us all out here on a wild-goose chase? Where's the Shark?'

Barney doesn't have a watch and he doesn't know about my tight and tidy schedule of events. He's unaware that his arrival is the first event. He's just driving a tractor and the police have not stopped him. The Shark has not slipped off the back. The engine has not broken down and he's almost there. Barney does the lap of honour and chugs the Shark past the Territorial Army Headquarters and the Headington Fire Station and heads to the heart of lace curtain land. A solitary man on a singular journey takes another swig of coffee, turns the corner into New High Street and runs smack into this circus. He screeches to a halt. Everyone goes silent. The Shark is about to begin.

The sculpture arriving at my house is a war baby. On the day she is conceived President Reagan sends the order for US planes based in the rural English countryside to attack Tripoli – yes this is 1986. During the night Colonel Gaddafi's daughter, Hannah, is killed, and two of his young sons end up in the emergency unit of a children's hospital in another of America's 'small wars'. On the morning of 15th April, Libyans who live in residential areas like mine wake up to find their homes smashed, their roofs with gaping holes and their families dead. On such a day the Shark takes shape.

I go to bed around midnight listening to the roar of F-111 squadrons leaving Upper Heyford airbase twenty miles north of Oxford, and get up to news reports of the air raids, wave after wave of bombers attacking military targets. By lunchtime the bulletins lead with the attacks on civilians and the destruction of the French Embassy. Bombs are dropping on the residential district of Bin Ashur in Tripoli where bodies are pulled out of the rubble when I visit my solicitor at noon, sign the deeds and buy my house, just another notch tucked safely away in the suburban belt around Oxford.

I wander through the bare rooms and start to plug in my appliances. The television reports at six o'clock show the scenes of devastation in this Libyan nightmare with houses burning, roofs precariously poised and families quietly in shock or screaming as they look for lost loved ones. It is a bitter-sweet day. I have the keys to my new house. I'm master in this piece of middle-terraced England, a space where I can call the shots. I'm safe in this little bit of my own dream, but I don't feel like celebrating.

3

BREAKING NEWS

OXFORD MAIL

TUESDAY, APRIL 15, 1986

AMERICA BOMBS LIBYA

Reagan sends in jets to punish Gaddafi

Rescuers search the ruins of buildings hit during the attack on Tripoli

The Penultimate Picture Palace with its giant
Al Jolson hands (top).

Not the Moulin Rouge (above) with its
eye-catching, high-kicking can-can legs.

Co-conspirator John Buckley (above).

John Buckley, a long-time friend since university days and a sculptor of some repute, comes by. I had collaborated with him on a few art-house cinema projects in Oxford when we painted the Penultimate Picture Palace façade black and attached white fibreglass eyes, lips, bowtie and hands to create a 3-D image of Al Jolson based on the poster for the first talkie, *The Jazz Singer*. We also worked on the Moulin Rouge Cinema where John had sculpted an outsized set of can-can legs high kicking

from the roof. Happily no one identified them as the legs of his tax inspector. Together John and I have 'form' when it comes to art and architecture.

With four bottles of Veuve Cliquot we walk outside to soak up the dying rays of sunshine across the road from the house. 'It's a bit ordinary.' John tends to be judgemental about other people's houses, possibly because he lives in a High Gothic Victorian lodge at the entrance to a cemetery. Is it envy or distain? 'Yes, but it's my bit of ordinary. I've always wanted to fit in, just never managed it . . . till now. I haven't owned a house before. I love the little green gate, the pink tea rose bushes and the front door with frosted glass panels. It's all so innocent. People can walk by and think "a nice family must live there".'

John jumps for the jugular. 'Since when were you innocent?' We know each other well enough to be comfortable with silences. I take a long drink of the champagne. 'Maybe it does need something.' We sit down on the pavement, using the ground as a table for the bottles of Veuve Cliquot and the glasses. The sun sinks, but an energy rises in the air. Even through the bouquet of the wine a whiff of destruction hangs around the day.

'How about the roof?' he asks, a little too much like Oliver Twist wanting more. I know exactly what he means, but I ignore that. 'It's splendid, a great canvas. Did you see that barn in the village of Swerford with a round peace symbol drawn on the tiles? The US airplanes from Upper Heyford have to fly over it for take off and landing. It's a nice gesture alongside all those hardened hangars on the base for planes with their nuclear payloads.'

John stamps on this one. 'Well we certainly don't want a gimmick that people can tuck away in a box in their brain and forget.'

'Perhaps we could hang a piece of sculpture over the door, like an unidentifiable melted shape.' I suggest something surreal like Salvador Dali's dripping watch redesigned as an improvised explosive device. 'It's derivative,' he retorts, 'we can do better. How about a horse on the roof?'

The heat-hazed visions of John Buckley that were to transform into the Headington Shark.

I need to know where this one comes from, where it's going and whether or not he plans to turn my house into a carousel.

John travels somewhere inside his memory. 'I was hitch-hiking on the shore of the Red Sea from Egypt to the Sudan. It was desolate. No birds, no wild life, except for a pack of wild dogs I could hear in the distance by day. During the night I thought they might attack. I was pretty much stranded with no traffic on the two-lane blacktop in a landscape of black rocks. The temperature was forty-five degrees day after day. The heat haze made the light shimmer and flicker. It wasn't a mirage, but I saw, or thought I saw, this beautiful horse, an Arabian stallion, rise up on the beach in the surf. It didn't belong. It was next to magic and completely out of kilter.'

I can be pretty judgemental too. 'I like the "almost magic moment", but if we have a horse people can still say "We know what that is" and dismiss it. This one doesn't have the bite.' John picks up on this. 'Funny you should mention bite because after the horse in the water, I went for a swim to get out of the bleached and black dry desert and into the wet world underneath. After swimming only a few metres the picture was completely different just below the surface – pink and purple polka-dot fish, yellow and blue striped fish, parrotfish with beaks to pick at the coral reefs, mantra rays and sharks. What about an image of a horse being eaten by a shark with the front legs still galloping while the back part is in the mouth and down the throat of some Great White?'

He is putting flesh on the idea . . . or ripping it off. 'I see where you're coming from. We live in a time where the unthinkable can . . . does happen; so why not a shark coming out of the sea to gobble a galloping horse? I like the shark idea. Can we do anything with that?' I ask.

John is back in his travels:

The first shark that got a hold of my imagination was a hammerhead. I was crewing on a yacht in the Pacific off Mexico. It wasn't a happy time. This group didn't do anything by the book, not that I minded. But I sunk the dug-out canoe which served as a dinghy. So when we needed to get some important documents to shore, everyone knew who should go overboard to swim with them. We dropped anchor about two hundred metres from the beach. It was mid-day. The sun pierced the clear water and we could see everything, including the shoal of thirty or forty hammerhead sharks that were circling the boat. They are the most menacing shape – fish from Mars but very fond of Earthling flesh. I waited. Well, what do you do when you have a nightmare? You wait. It will pass . . . probably.'

This is beginning to sound like a horror story; and I didn't realise John had so many lying just below the surface. He continues:

Our crew packaged the documents in a waterproof pouch and decided I should deliver them on shore. It was one of those "English" decisions – no vote, no discussion, except everyone knows whose head is on the block. After half an hour I dived in and swam. In my head the two hundred metres were two hundred years. I made it through, probably to the intense annoyance of the rest of the crew, and handed over the documents.

People don't swim in shark-infested waters twice . . . normally. I had no choice. The return trip to the yacht seemed interminable. I don't know how I survived. The problem was not the hammerhead shark shoal somewhere out there. No, the anxiety existed inside my head. Imagination is lord of reality, that's certain. I had to face the biggest fear of my life, the fear of not knowing when I will be attacked or where or indeed whether it will happen, but all the time knowing that I am in immediate and intense danger.'

John Buckley's nightmares of shark-infested waters: *'I had to face the biggest fear of my life, the fear of not knowing when I will be attacked or where or indeed whether it will happen . . .'*

John is quiet for a moment. 'Can I rip open your roof?' He catches me off-guard. Is this John's version of a shark attack on me? 'What exactly do you have in mind?' I reply trying to recover my composure. 'Instead of a shark jumping out of the water, how about a shark diving into your roof? We tell the story with the tail. Get rid of all the obvious bits. Leave that to the imagination . . . like this.' John produces a biro and draws a sketch on a scrap of paper. It's powerful and yet playful. I can imagine small versions bobbing up and down in children's bathtubs and larger versions dropping on Japanese cities during the final days of World War II. 'It works. Where do we go from here?' All this happens in fifteen minutes. By the end of our conversation the shark's tail is already twitching.

'Instead of a shark jumping out of the water, how about a shark diving into your roof?'

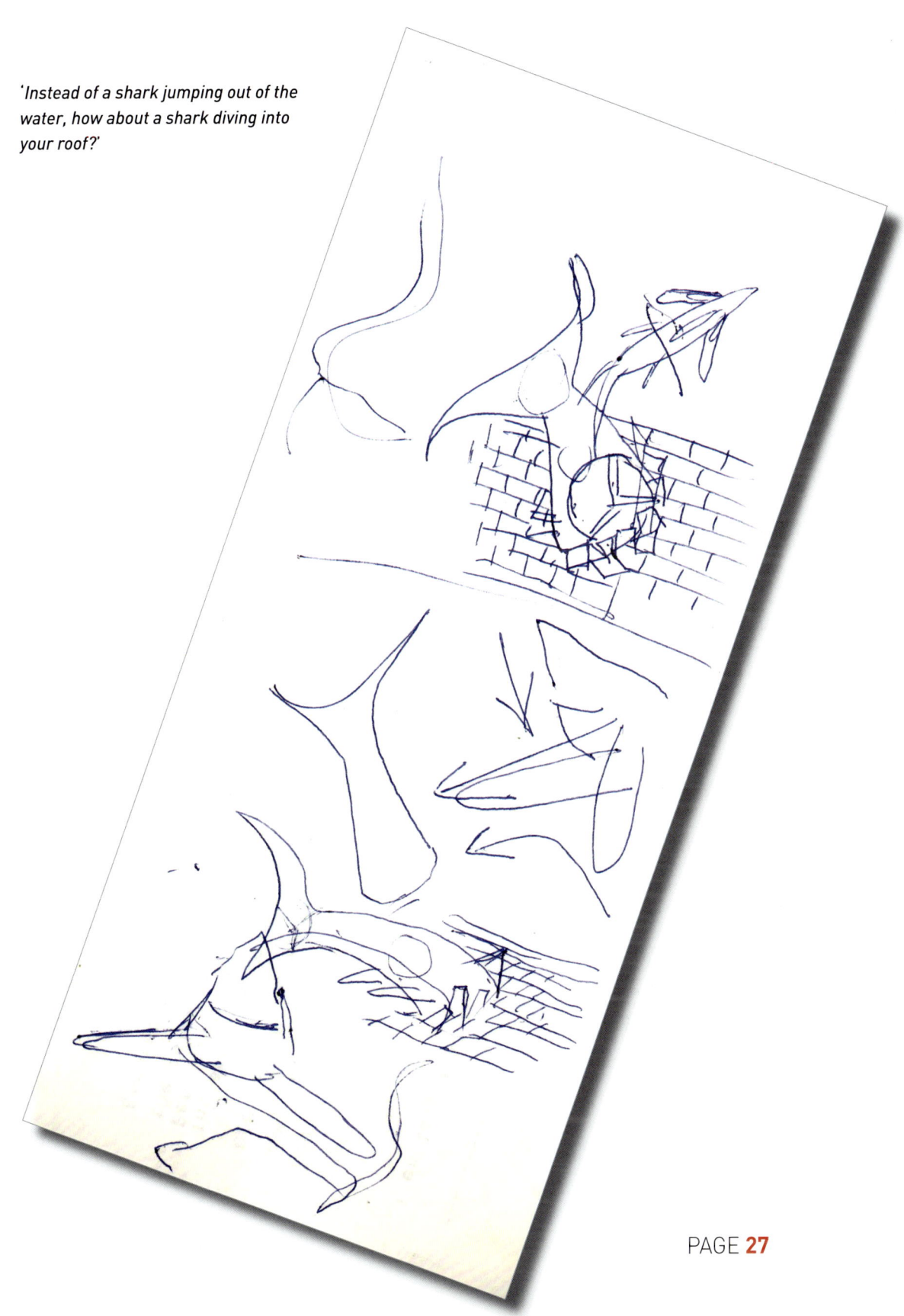

Left: And what rough beast, its hour come round at last, is about to be born? The first time the Shark (top) hits the roof.

'You're lowering the tone of the street!' My neighbours are twitching now. Irene Williams, an elderly resident with a voice like a bull, starts to bellow. 'Nobody has a thing like that in their rooftop, do they . . . except . . . are you mad or something? This is a private residential area. We don't have sharks in our roofs here. It's disgusting. That shark should be down at the seaside, not in a rooftop. You'd have been better, far better off, taking a nice pose of my voluptuous body and putting it on the top of your house.'

Mrs Williams is four and a half feet high and more than three feet wide and often sports an outsized white plastic handbag hooked on her right elbow, but maybe she does have a point. An image of her stuck headlong in a hole in my roof with her legs aloft and akimbo might be more in keeping with the tone of New High Street.

'The shark doesn't worry me in any way at all,' says Mrs Bagshaw. 'But I think it's a pity you just didn't put a white dove for peace up there. That's all I've got to say about it.' Whether a twenty-five foot white dove would have placated Mrs Bagshaw remains to be seen . . . I want to pick her up on the dove idea. If she's looking for comfort and reassurance, then of course she will be disturbed by anything but the bland and familiar. Most of the important art of this century is a transgression that disrupts the warm blanket of our dove-loving habits. But this is not the time.

Two cranes are blocking off the road now and operators tie a piece of rubber around the Shark's tail to protect it from the lifting rope. Slowly the sculpture floats off away from Mrs Williams and Mrs Bagshaw who follow the winch with open mouths and stand right under the 'flight path'. This is dangerous, especially when the Shark is not only dangling, wiggling and waving in the wind, but spinning violently as it goes higher than the house to avoid ripping out the electricity cables in the street.

I know I should clear the area and we need to remove the parked cars in case the four-hundredweight sculpture has an unexpected landing. But there's no time for that. It's all happening, higher and higher, above the chimney pots and the trees. This is getting tense. For me it's pretty much torture. As the Shark rises inch by inch I can feel a hot blade sink into the back of my brain, inch by inch. An eerie silence swallows the crowd and I turn round to catch their reactions. An old man limps along the street opposite. He glances at the people, follows their gaze and squints at the house. Then he looks away quickly. 'I don't want to see that,' he mutters to no one in particular. He is alone. 'I've seen it all before. I was there, in London during the blitz. I saw the bombs. I felt the fire. I heard the screams. That's destructive and dangerous, and it almost killed me once. I know what it's all about and I don't need it now.'

He is so quiet and dignified that almost no one hears. I see him walk away sadly, shaking his head. He knew. He saw through.

The postman does not. When Mr David MacDonald comes round the corner of New High Street to deliver mail, he stops and stares and drops his bag full of letters. This trusted public servant runs home to get his wife and child and camera and comes back to take a picture of the 'freak accident'. Mr MacDonald doesn't see the motley crew desperately and inexpertly trying to bring the Shark into the house. He thinks they are trying to pull it out. 'I wonder how long it will take?' he asks his five-year-old daughter. 'To do what?' she answers . . . .

There is some commotion in the crowd. A large man is running through the throng holding the hand of an elderly woman. He shouts to her in an Arkansas accent: 'Come on Mabel, I want you to see just how crazy the English can be . . .'

I look up to get my bearings on this 'Is-it-landing-or-leaving' debate, and see members of the team struggling. A former marine seismologist is frantically tearing out tiles and doing a great job of smashing them. This does look like both an entrance and an exit. Has he snapped under the pressure of installing the Shark?

I escape from the crowd to investigate. Looking from the inside of the roof at this surreal Shark spinning into infinity just above the ridge tiles, I see it can't land because the hole in the roof is too tiny. It's only a small detail. 'Rip up some more tiles. When I've lost fifty, five or ten here or there don't matter.'

From the roof-top vantage point, I see trouble brewing. It's 9:00 a.m. and the police finally hear that a suspicious Shark is floating over a hole in a house. They are on my tail. Two 'bobbies' have turned up in a panda car. The police driver jams on the breaks, drops her jaw and clamps eyes on the sculpture. The other 'bobby' rolls down his window, half way, takes out a notebook and asks me to explain what I am doing. 'Just putting a shark in my roof.'

The policeman looks at his blank paper in silence, trying to think of something to say. 'Have you ever done this before?' 'No, officer, this is my first time.' Since there is no law against putting a Shark through a roof, he rolls up his window with the deliberate motion of a turtle going back into its shell, and the panda car wends its way through the crowd.

Mr Pitt is furious. Mr Pitt is a plumber in his prime who lives opposite with his father at number nine. 'That's no way to talk to the police. Don't you have any respect for them at all? You can't say to a policeman "I'm just putting a Shark in my roof!" That's absurd. It's rude. You can't treat the British bobby like that. How dare you stick that Shark there anyway? You've broken the rules. You live in this street. It's not just your home; it's our home. We all have to share this space. You have to face your neighbours every day. You have an obligation to them and now you've done this. You don't deserve to be part of the community.'

'Yes, Mr Pitt, we have to face our neighbours, but we also have to face our nightmares. Every era has an image that confronts its intimate fears and fantasies, and the sight of a house invaded by what some are calling 'a bomb' touches our worst fear. The sculpture works because the potential destruction of the house plays upon fundamental insecurities that you and I both share. It is disturbing, and that's the point.'

Muriel Pimm puts her oar in. 'That animal is a time replica of the most voracious of all the fish in the sea. It would be quite acceptable in the East End of London, but not in one of the finest cities in the world. Of course, I refer to our University and our famous buildings. Even our enemies in the last World War respected Oxford and kept the bombs away from the area. When foes show respect it is regrettable that those who live here do not have the same regard.'

I need an antidote to this antagonism and head back into the house. The atmosphere inside is completely different. People are positively buzzing, but with an edge. Something else is amiss. I climb to the attic where the second fly in this Shark's ointment is obvious.

It's a detail with a difference. The Shark has three long, angle iron struts embedded inside its fibreglass frame that will slot into three areas of the metal base already constructed in the attic. The Shark will be welded onto the base of reinforced steel joists which are connected to the four walls of the house so all the strain will be channelled down to the ground-floor pilings. Simple, right? Except the metal struts in the Shark don't match up with the slots in the base. This mistake means it's not possible to weld the sculpture in place.

There's a moment when the surreal becomes chaotic, when the nightmare becomes real and you can feel the cold claws grab the base of your skull and rip down your spine. This is that moment. I want to scream, but I can't; that would frighten the team . . . even more.

The welder, Bob Luff, is desperately trying to break off a strut with the hacksaw so at least the Shark can enter the roof void. But what are we going to do in the long term? It's like working on a jigsaw puzzle with some key pieces missing. We could keep the Shark dangling over the house for two days until Monday when we can correct the fault. We could lower the Shark to the ground and admit defeat, or we could bodge it. Luffy has been making nooses most of his life and the harpsichord maker Mark Waddington is also a sailor with experience of nautical knots, so they go for the only option, grab some rope and lasso the Shark onto the roof.

Just _ when you thought it was safe to go shopping

Rooftop Jaws leaves the locals gasping

A larger-than-life Jaws that just dropped in on a Headington house has baffled and amused local people.

People living in New High Street were amazed on Saturday morning to see a 25ft glass fibre model of a great white shark sticking out of the roof of the home of cinema boss Mr William Heine.

Shocked neighbours were woken by the noise of a crane winching the giant of the deep into place opposite Mr Heine's other bizarre sculpture — the can-can dancing legs which ornament his cinema, Not the Moulin Rouge.

And the question everyone was asking was: "Why the most feared of all sharks?"

"If he is doing if for a joke, when is it all going to stop? We had enough trouble over the high-kicking legs," said Mrs Jenny Pitt, who lives a few doors away from Mr Heine.

"But you have to laugh about it — anyone flying overhead might think this is Disneyland."

Passers-by Peter and Barry Churchman of Barton Road, Headington, said they were shocked when they saw the oceanic predator and thought it was a silly stunt.

The shark, which weighs four hundredweight, was commissioned by Mr Heine from artist John Buckley, who also designed the legs.

Even after Mr Heine said there was a serious anti-war and anti-nuclear message in the eye-catching sculpture, onlookers were still bemused.

"A bomb sticking out of his roof would have made more sense," Mrs Pitt said.

But other people were hooked on Mr Heine's fishy folly.

"I think it is a great idea," said Mr Steve Rawlings of New High Street. "It is something different and cheers the place up."

Many people took snapshots of the novelty sculpture which is certain to cause a row with local planners.

Mrs Christine Peck of Valentia Road, Headington, couldn't see any harm in it.

"After putting up the legs at the cinema, Mr Heine might have come up with something naughtier than a fish," she said.

Dr Nigel Key, who also lives in Headington, thought it was a "hilarious" but expensive stunt.

It took workmen most of Saturday morning to fix the giant sculpture in place, its nose disappearing into a jagged hole in the roof and its body angled precariously, as if the shark had fallen from the sky.

Steel girders were positioned in the house loft to take the weight of the sculpture. But some confused onlookers thought it was all an accident.

Shoppers Mrs Elsie Johnson and Mrs Molly Stayte, who live in Stapleton Road nearby, thought it was all a bit silly and a waste of money.

"Fancy wrecking the roof of your house with a giant fish!" said Mrs Stayte.

'Please dad, let's get out of here' . . . 22-months-old Erin and father Dr Nigel Key

'Something fishy about this' . . . Lauretta and Ronald Patrick of Latimar Road, Headington pass by

Elsie Johnson and Molly Stayte . . . all a bit silly, they thought

'It's no joke: like Chernobyl'

MR BILL Heine, the man responsible for the shark on the rooftop insists that it should not be taken as a joke.

"This is not something we dreamed up in August as a silly season story to make headlines," he said.

"The shark was to express someone feeling totally impotent and ripping a hole in their roof out of a sense of impotence and anger and desperation."

He chose Saturday to put up the model because it was the forty first anniversary of the day the atomic bomb was dropped on Nagasaki.

"John and I did this to ask a question. It is saying something about CND, nuclear power, Chernobyl and Nagasaki. It isn't just something to make people laugh.

In a printed statement which Mr Heine handed out to passers-by he said: "Everyone lives in a work of art. The trouble is that they are such repetitive works. I call my house Untitled 1986. It is simply an addition to the street of rather dull art works.

"I bought it in April on the day the United States bombed Tripoli. Somehow having a huge shark smashing through one's roof seems to be the consistent thing to do. It's so sensible. It breaks through into the heart of the home like rain from Chernobyl."

A field day for the local press and a photo-opportunity (above) with an inappropriate caption trying to mix 'terrified child' with dangerous shark.

I smile for the cameras (top right), uncertain as to whether I am in the eye of the storm or in the calm before . . .

The _Oxford Mail_ editors didn't believe reporter Chris Gray when he first told them about the Shark, but they eventually got the picture (opposite).

PAGE **32**

Local residents in shock about the Shark.

All images courtesy of the Oxford Mail/Oxford Times (Newsquest Oxfordshire)

Over the next hour this versatile team ties the sculpture from the lattice steel work inside it to the floor with a yachting 'bottle screw', the kind that keeps the mast upright on a boat. For belt and braces safety they also tie it to the four walls so it can still lean over the footpath and yet be secure. You can't tell there is any problem from the outside but however you slice this one the Shark is hanging by a shoestring, a professionally tied, state-of-the-art, tried and tested shoestring. It is almost impossible to enter or leave the 'Shark room' because these ropes fill the space like a giant piece of macramé that would do justice to Heath Robinson.

The crunch time comes when the crane loosens its grip on the Shark. Only then do we know if the sculpture stands or falls. Of course there never really is an Armageddon moment like that, at least not in England because everything happens so gradually.

The winch from the crane slowly comes down and loosens the tension on the rope holding the Shark to the crane while at the same time tightening the tension on the other rope holding the Shark to the house. It is great, tense teamwork, akin to that of trapeze artists bending and swaying into hand-stands and somersaults and landing elegantly on their feet. The crane is now completely detached. The Shark lands safely on her 'head'.

John Buckley (leaning against his sculpture) and Bill Heine (houseowner, right) raise their glasses to the Shark in anticipation of the battle with Oxford City Council as to whether it's an eyesore or a work of art.

PART TWO

THEATRE OF THE ABSURD

DATELINE: 15TH OCTOBER, 1986

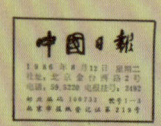 **CHINA DAILY**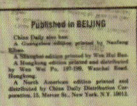

Vol. 6 No. 1575 · Tuesday, August 12, 1986 · 2 Jintai Xilu, Beijing · Tel. 595220 · Telex: 22022 CNDY CN · Price: 10 fen; 15 fen (airmail)

Neighbours stare at a 25-metre fibre glass shark sticking out of the roof of a house owned by Bill Heine in Headington, Oxford, England. Bill, a cinema owner, thought the addition would brighten up a rather dull street.

Bill,
See Back page.

With the compliments of

You even reached the China daily current in kabul, Afghanistan WELL DONE!

BRITISH EMBASSY KABUL

Peter Carter P.

On Her Britannic Majesty's Service

CODE No. 23-92

BILL HEINE
(SHARK ON THE ROOF)
HEADINGTON
OXFORD
UK.

Although the Shark is far from finished we down tools and celebrate for two days and nights, right through the lightning, thunder and rain. When I arrive back home at eight o'clock on Monday morning two inches of water are covering the floor tiles of my kitchen two storeys below the Shark.

6

The August downpours have come straight through the gaping hole in my roof, soaked the planks of the bedroom, dripped into the plaster ceiling beneath and turned the ground-floor kitchen into a giant bath tub. Don't panic. It's early enough to sort this out and get things back to normal, whatever that is. I put on a pair of wellies and survey the damage. I need time to think this through.

Immediately a bell rings, like a sound from one of those annoying radio programmes when you are confronted with a mission-impossible question and the thirty seconds are up; but maybe it's only the front door. I stick my head slowly into the hall and see through the frosted-glass windows a posse of seven people, one wearing the familiar helmet of a policeman, the others twitching too much to give away any identification clues. They certainly are not wearing wellies and the morning sun catches the shine from their shoes – bureaucrats!

After the third ring I hear another chime, slightly out of synch. Am I hallucinating? No it's the kitchen phone. I wade over to answer it so the posse won't hear. Terry Wogan's producer is on the line asking me to come to the BBC studios in London straight away and prepare to be a guest on his TV programme this evening. I whisper that I'm in pretty deep water at the moment. Could they call back later?

I resume the game of peek-a-boo with the bureaucrats now pounding on my front door. They get fed up after twenty minutes and leave, but it's like Noah's Ark down here because the tenants descend two by two for tea and toast. I enlist them in the effort to reclaim the kitchen while I go search for the Shark.

Up in the attic the sculpture has survived, intact and in place, tethered by ropes that haven't moved an inch; and yet the Shark has travelled round the world. The morning mail includes a letter that says 'On Her Britannic Majesties Service' via the diplomatic pouch from the Cultural Attaché at the British Embassy in Kabul enclosing a copy of the *China Daily*: 'BILL, See Back Page. You even reached the *China Daily* circuit in Kabul, Afghanistan WELL DONE!.'

Peter Hull from Auckland writes:

> *Your Shark appeared here on TV. So did your Moulin Rouge cinema*
> *and so did you. Saturday the Shark was on the main news-page of*

the newspaper. It says you did it to brighten an otherwise dull street. Congratulations!. I think it's brilliant. Quite the most creative idea I've seen for ages. Certainly the sort of thing one expects only from California. Every bit as good as and probably better than the rich man's follies of the previous century.

As you can see you've brightened up more than a dull street. You've brightened whole countries! Personally I think the eccentric people are the normal ones, it's the rest of them that are funny! Again, sincere congratulations on marvellous creativity and on beating the bureaucrats. You've given me a jawful experience.'

Closer to home Mrs Olivia Elworthy from North Oxford is equally adamant:

'There can be few as arrogant and chauvinistic as you, Mr Heine. Your sheer impudence and effrontery not to mention audacity is classic, coming as it does from an all-time law breaker. I ask whether we can all have an assortment of animals protruding from our roofs. If you can flout the law so can the rest of us. You should have been imprisoned to teach you a lesson. A fine example you are to the younger generations, acting like an overgrown schoolboy. I hope you are made to remove the animal.'

So the 'big idea' of the Shark is alive and kicking, but the small nuts and bolts bits are about to kill it. That posse will be back and the Building Control Officer of Oxford City Council has left a note. 'I have received a number of complaints from local people who are worried that the Shark could slip off the roof. Contact me immediately.'

This Shark is going to be a one-week wonder if we don't crack the problem of how to attach it to the house. But then we've got it up there. Maybe that's enough. After all nobody – not even the sculptor John Buckley or I – really expects it will stay there. The question is not if it will come down, but when.

We aren't slipping into defeat; we simply know from the start we'll never win. You can't beat City Hall.

It's been a great success, but on another level it has been a colossal failure – my house is a wreck. Do I really want to pay this price for having a Shark in my roof? We've made the point. We've asked the questions. Maybe it's time now to furl our flag, repair the roof and tug our forelocks. We've ripped through the order and structure of everyday life and provided a glimpse of something else. Perhaps we should leave it at that. Why go that next step to connect something in a permanent way to the house when we know in our heart of hearts that it's only temporary?

I wrestle with this question while I fight off Mr and Mrs Outraged of Oxford who do battle on every front and they don't take hostages. But to be fair the criticisms are creative.

Shark could be a killer! screams one headline, 'Residents claim it's only a matter of time before a pedestrian is mown down by a distracted driver.'

Neighbours under threat – 'Angle of sculpture leaning over the footpath makes it likely to topple onto the locals.'

Shark danger to tenants – 'People living in the house could be crushed by Shark when it sinks inside.'

In these days of outrage, accusation and hatred, something happens. I see how an early dawn-chorus of confusion and anger can grow from a tiny tweet into a terribly large cacophony with the passion and power to obliterate debate. And if nobody wants to listen we won't get to the conversation about what the Shark means. The initial hysteria against the sculpture produces an equal and opposite reaction from me.

I remember the advice of Aeneas when his city of Troy was sacked and burned. Trying to escape with an elderly father strapped on his back and holding his young son by the hand, he shouts to his supporters 'Our only hope is to have no hope.' I'm not trying to compare

An impassioned letter of support (right), typifying the personal responses I receive in the wake of the Shark's sudden appearance.

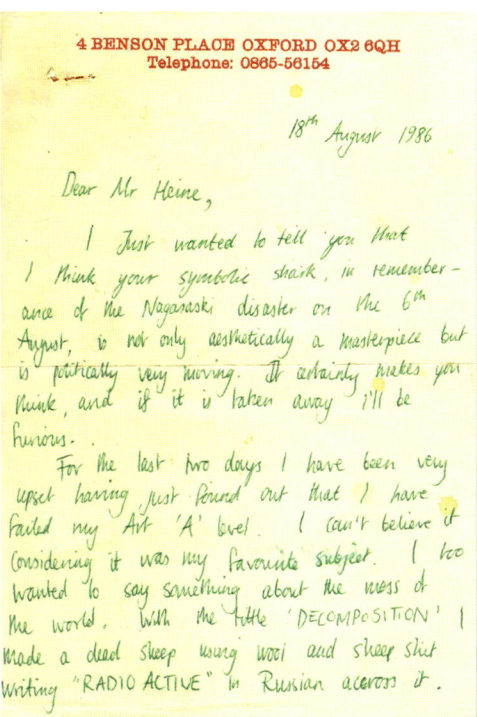

4 BENSON PLACE OXFORD OX2 6QH
Telephone: 0865-56154

18th August 1986

Dear Mr Heine,

I just wanted to tell you that I think your symbolic shark, in remembrance of the Nagasaki disaster on the 6th August, is not only aesthetically a masterpiece but is politically very moving. It certainly makes you think, and if it is taken away I'll be furious.

For the last two days I have been very upset having just found out that I have failed my Art 'A' level. I can't believe it considering it was my favourite subject. I too wanted to say something about the mess of the world. With the title 'DECOMPOSITION' I made a dead sheep using wool and sheep shit writing "RADIO ACTIVE" in Russian across it.

The Chernobyl accident had just happened and I felt very strongly about actually saying something through Art, rather than playing it safe with a water colour of my Grandmother or something! However.... They failed me ~ so don't let the bastards take away your shark.

I've driven up to see it twice today. Quite a tourist attraction! Perhaps the council should be paying you!!

Best of luck,

from a great admirer,

Emily Fuller

myself with anyone else; I'm simply saying that even if you are going to lose that's no reason not to fight, especially if you get to present the arguments during the fight.

I don't have a hope in hell, but I'm going to give it a damn good go, and who knows, tomorrow when I wake I might be on another part of this journey and see the sun rise from a different angle and find a new possibility.

One of the best structural engineers in the country who has written the classic textbook on his subject gives me advice. He visits the Shark house, does the calculations and suggests a few tweaks to the sculpture. After following his instructions we are able to take away the Heath Robinson ropes. The Shark is done and my structural engineer, Jack Dawson, says that sixty years is the normally accepted timescale for building structures to last.

I open my door to the Building Control Officer at eleven o'clock in the morning. He spends almost an hour inspecting the four-hundredweight sculpture fixed to my roof and takes away the drawings. I collect from his office the officially approved safety certificate before five o'clock the same day, probably the fastest record from application to approval in the history of the Oxford City Council Building Control Department. But the bureaucrats are not best pleased. I hear the disappointment in their voices and catch a flash of steel in their eyes.

All the signals are there. They are in attack mode and they have been defeated now and for the next sixty years at the first hurdle. If Oxford City Council wants to remove the Shark by whatever means possible then let the battle begin.

We treat the Shark operation like a military manoeuvre that requires undercover activity. We spring it by surprise on an unsuspecting populace. I agree to every step of secrecy but each one goes against the grain of my DNA. My neighbours have a right to know that I am making their ordinary street unfamiliar. I'm dropping a symbol of natural violence into suburban domestic security. I'm changing my house fundamentally – with its brick bay windows, gate, garden, lace curtains and everything beyond those curtains that the imagination can create – into a plinth for an object that challenges all other elements of the house and leads beyond the slippers under the easy chair to a deeper and darker place.

7

THE MAD HATTER'S TEA PARTY

People in New High Street wanted to wake up on 9th August, 1986 and see things as they always were – knowable, comfortable and secure. I'm pulling the rug out from under that reality without so much as a 'by your leave'. I don't believe in doing that, but I do it anyway.

If I consult my neighbours I will have to describe this transformation, and I don't have the words or experience to say what the Shark will do to them. My words would at least deform the sculpture and probably destroy it. This is something that needs to live, to be seen, before it can be judged. The Shark doesn't fit into the convenient classification of the English planning system. We're going outside the box, and we don't know if anyone else will follow. So mum's the word and the Shark is a shock.

Nevertheless approval is important, and I do want to make amends; so I invite my neighbours and the Oxford City Councillors to discuss it at a tea party. The invite goes as follows:

> 'By now some of you may know that New High Street has a "New" piece of sculpture – a Shark crashing through the roof of my house. The person who created the sculpture is internationally recognized artist John Buckley and his work has been exhibited around the world from the Museum of Modern Art in Paris to New York, Amsterdam and the kingdom of Oman. This Shark in our street is intended as a piece of visual surprise designed to delight and to disturb. Judging from comments by local residents, I gather the sculpture has succeeded in doing just that: many of you are delighted . . . many of you are disturbed. John Buckley and I have made our statement by presenting you with this piece of sculpture. Now it is time for us to listen to your statements.
>
> We would like to hear what you have to say about the Shark because we

PAGE **43**

really are interested in your reactions; and we wish to invite you to come
and meet the newest local resident in our street at a tea party on Sunday,
31st August from 4.00 to 6.00. We very much hope you will be able to
attend. I appreciate that there may be one or two of you who might wish to
compare this tea party with something out of Alice in Wonderland! Indeed,
I myself thought it would be fun to call this the Mad Hatter's Tea Party, so
if any of you would like to come in fancy dress, please feel free.'

It doesn't take long for this ball to bounce. Both Councillors and neighbours grab the opportunity to shake my hand or punch me in the nose. On a positive note one neighbour writes: 'A short Shark shock was much needed in a drab area. It is the only thing worth looking at this side of Magdalen College. The road should be renamed Shark Street. Please don't let anyone take it away. I know it is meant to have a serious meaning, but it paradoxically is cheering everyone up. People have even started talking to each other! (But how do you keep the rain out of your roof?)'

I am not prepared to discuss the rain and my roof because I don't want to let that particular cat out of the bag. I'm still scratching my head on that one and praying for dry weather on the tea party afternoon. If it rains the guests will be in for a shock.

A tea party, especially a Mad Hatter's Tea Party should be a fun event, where guests are polite, civil, smiling even and prepared to enjoy themselves. This is a tea party with a difference. The weather is warm outside the house, inside the atmosphere is icy. My neighbours arrive with all the ease and bonhomie of a health visitor entering a leper colony. They keep their arms folded for fear of touching a door knob and getting a disease. I serve them English tea, Irish coffee, Welsh punch or a wee dram of something Scottish and I even pass around a comments book. Entries range from: 'It's brill', to 'You've more tiles missing than your roof.'

Usually at events like this it takes a while to break the ice, but not here. Each of my neighbours arrives with a sledge hammer, and they begin swinging as soon as they can corner their target – me. Dr Laurence Harwood of No. 7 has a high voice when he's rattled: 'It's an act of cheap sensationalism and it's devaluing the street. People who live away from this area think the Shark's marvellous. For many of us who live here, it's a tasteless monstrosity. The influx of gawpers has destroyed the privacy of locals and makes life hell for the residents of Alison Clay House sheltered accommodation in the street, many of whom are infirm. Our peace and privacy are at stake and we do not intend to give in easily. Be warned.'

Mrs Irene Williams of the aforementioned sheltered housing adds her voice describing the sculpture as 'an eyesore. If Mr Heine wants to spend his money, why doesn't he spend it on helping the hospitals and the needy? He should never have got away with this.'

Mr Peter Pitt of No. 9 also takes a practical stand. 'If I want to sell my house, what are prospective buyers going to think when they see that thing?'

Mrs June Whitehouse is more philosophical 'It's not causing an inconvenience. It doesn't smell and it doesn't make a noise. I like it.' And she produces this poem:

Hark Hark – the Shark
From Heine hath come
Into New High Street's classy aplomb.
Stretcheth to sky
Puzzleth passers-by
A reminder to all of the bomb.
O warlike fish –
Bring peace to our street
As we look up, smile, and pass on.

Not everyone can take tea with The Mad Hatter. Councillor Bill Fagg, a one-time Lord Mayor of Oxford sends more than his 'regrets' (above).

June is one of several poets who perform. Over two hundred people pack into my house and overflow into the garden where people queue up to bend my ear, including the Cheshire Cat, the Red Queen, Tweedledum and Tweedledee. The party eventually goes with a swing as unusual bedfellows get to know each other. There isn't much dialogue and some shouting, but not enough to disturb the dormouse. I think they all enjoy it in spite of themselves, but one thing is certain: this particular Hatter will never throw a Mad Tea Party again.

How mad does this battle get? And more to the point, who fires the first shot? That's debatable. I don't apply to Oxford City Council for planning permission because the Shark is none of their business. This little act is a big thing in the Council's view – the equivalent of throwing a hand grenade through the planning regulations, their first line of defence against chaos.

The omission triggers an onslaught from the Planners and they react like a singed adder: 'A Shark? Through the roof? He can't do that! Off with its head, immediately! We must be able to control this.' They put in a planning application on my behalf. This gives them the opportunity to 'carry out the usual public consultation and advertisement'.

Battle lines are drawn. The opposition attacks with an eight-point plan generated from 'the consultation':

Visual Appearance. 'The Shark is ugly and an eyesore and makes an otherwise pleasant suburban street look like a less salubrious bit of an inner city. It is vulgar, in bad taste and in conflict with the character of New High Street.'

Disregard for the Feelings and Rights of others. 'The reason for the erection of the Shark is to defy and ridicule the law abiding public and the Planning Committee. The act is akin to football hooliganism in that it displays a total disregard for the feelings and rights of others. It is evident that Mr Heine will continue with his cavalier disregard for the law and his neighbours until checked.'

Precedent. 'If the Shark is allowed there will be nothing in principle to stop any of the inhabitants erecting 'works of art' on their houses. In fact, comments have already been heard which suggest that if Mr Heine gets away with the Shark he has even more bizarre plans to be implemented at some future time.'

Erection without Planning Permission. It was resented that the Shark was erected without planning permission. 'If the Shark is allowed to remain how can the Planning Committee pass judgement on the merits of a mundane house extension or similar alterations to property in this area in the future?'

Reduction in House Values. 'The Shark may reduce the saleable value of the houses near it. Due to this effect there should be a tax reduction for properties in the immediate vicinity.'

Traffic. 'Congestion and several near-miss accidents have been created by slow moving sight-seers.'

► **Likelihood of it Becoming Unsafe.** 'After a period of exposure to the elements it is not unlikely that the whole structure could become unsafe and liable to cause damage to property and a risk to life – especially in a freak gale?'

► **On the Town Hall.** 'Would Planning Committee give permission for the erection of the Shark in any road where individual members live or even on the Town Hall?'

I understand the public outcry but the planners have no legal basis to go to war over it. I know this probably hurts the egos of local politicians who are champing at the bit to bite the Shark's head off but local authorities should not try to impose their tastes in aesthetic matters. I walk into the Committee meeting, look them in the eye and lay it on the line: 'The Planning Acts are not intended to control public art. It is not the purpose of planning legislation to set up politicians as judges of taste and artistic standards. This would give some amateur hacks on the Planning Committee the power to decide what art is suitable or unsuitable for people like you and me. Worse, it would give them the power to restrict public access to new ideas, and that isn't acceptable in this day and age.'

Just how far do the local politicians support local democracy? 'Any system that puts control over artistic matters in their hands means that a small band of politicos, unqualified in any aspect of building design, can enforce their particular prejudices. It would be arbitrary and absurd to concentrate even more power in fewer, fumbling hands.'

The Committee Members bristle when I bring up Berlin. 'A group of aesthetic gauleiters setting standards of art and architecture amounts to a type of political censorship and the main argument against that is enshrined in the artistic debacle of the Third Reich.'

I sense I'm digging my own grave with my tongue, but I haven't reached Moscow yet. 'It would be surreal to surrender artistic control to a committee. Most people agree that while committees might be helpful in providing a local government that can collect the rubbish on time, they are less than useful in creating a piece of art. The recent Soviet forays into this area indicate that art by committee is a recipe for ruin.'

Somebody has to put the case for the artist.

'If we value public sculpture the artist must have a free hand in creating public art. What nonsense for any sculptor to give one group or individual a veto or censorship power over public art, because the most exciting aspect of something like the Shark nose-diving into my roof is that it belongs to everyone, not just to one person or group.

It is a creation for the whole community and the artist is the trustee to balance the hopes and fears of that community.

The sculpture is not a planning matter but simply an integrated part of the design of the building and maintains and improves the aesthetic standard of the house. The Shark is part and parcel of the natural growth of our visual environment in much the same way that carvings, gargoyles and sculpture have always contributed to the development of a more humane and pleasant place to live.

We are fortunate that painters and sculptors in the past like Leonardo da Vinci and Michelangelo didn't have to submit their works to a "hanging committee" for approval.'

I think that phrase does it – completely quashes any hope of Planning Committee support for the Shark. There is silence for a second and then the sound of foot solders marching in unison. Committee chairman Andrew Smith says:

'It has been a very imaginative and successful publicity stunt which has given a good laugh, not just to people in Oxford but to others all over the world. But I understand the attitude of people who say that this joker is getting away with something like this, so why can't we?'

Fellow Labour councillor John Power is more direct in his attack on me:

'In any self-respecting country he would have been locked up years ago. You can't have someone smashing a hole in a roof and saying he is making a gesture for peace when he chooses a sculpture of the most violent and savage creature on earth.'

This is pretty much an open and shut case. The Members recommend that the Shark requires planning permission and 'the Committee would not have been minded to grant planning permission for the Shark, had an application been submitted by Mr Heine'; and they authorise the Council's legal officer to 'take enforcement action to bring about the removal of the Shark from the roof of 2 New High Street in six months' time'.

The Shark is done and dusted. . . and dead.

'Let's be absolutely frank about this. The man is a nutcase.'

The Planning Committee has recommended harpooning the roof-top Shark. However, it may still survive because the full council has the final word. Although Oxford City Council usually rubber-stamps the Committees' reports, all Members have an option to accept or reject them. We could still turn this fight around.

An unassuming suburban street transformed and lit up.

I fire off a few salvos: 'The Great White Shark will certainly have a reaction to the death warrant. It may turn purple with outrage.' I have a cunning plan and the Committee misunderstand it. They demand to know if I intend to paint over the naturalistic colours and put a new coat on the Shark. I can smell a whiff of paranoia here with talk of the Shark and its Technicolor dream coat.

I continue on another, definitely more convenient, and possibly pompous, tack: 'Through its decision to destroy the sculpture the Planning Committee has taken the plunge into deep water and probably beyond the bounds of its power. I welcome this opportunity to take the matter to the law courts and clarify whether there is still some freedom left where art and architecture can brighten the dull environment in which we live.'

The lines are drawn but in this battle a fifth column infiltrates the council side. The Labour Leader of the Council, Alan Griffiths, praises the Shark as 'a serious work of art which has entertainment value. Individuals have rights and artists have rights and it is inappropriate for local councils to interfere. Mr Heine has been pulling our leg very successfully, and I move we allow him to get on with it.'

His colleague, Labour member John Power disagrees, 'That's the most irresponsible contribution to a debate I've heard in a long time.' He dismisses 'all this rubbish about art. Let's be absolutely frank about this. The man is a nutcase. A nutcase. Mr Heine has made it absolutely clear that this is a publicity stunt through and through. We have got to insist it comes down.'

The Shark even manages to unite Oxford City Councillors who are usually at each other's throats. The Conservative Leader, Major General John Stanyer, agrees with his Labour colleague John Power: 'Mr Heine is making a V-for-Victory sign to this Committee. He's one of those individuals who want their own way without any concern for other people. We are being taken for a ride. This has been fun while it lasted but what next? Is the Shark going to have a family? We can't have Sharks being erected in roofs in Oxford. It's not Blackpool front. It's not Disneyland.'

This back-slapping cross-party agreement is not lost on one Oxford resident: 'It is interesting that art has united leading members of both of our great political parties and thus has reached parts that mere politics could not. What cuts across political ideology is a shared determination to impose conformity.'

But another Conservative councillor, Ann Spokes, is 'unashamedly pro-Shark' and describes the sculpture as a 'sleek and beautiful creature'.

This Shark is already wending its way through to the hearts and minds of some hard-bitten politicians, and the longer it remains on my roof the more powerful that connection becomes. I need to play for time.

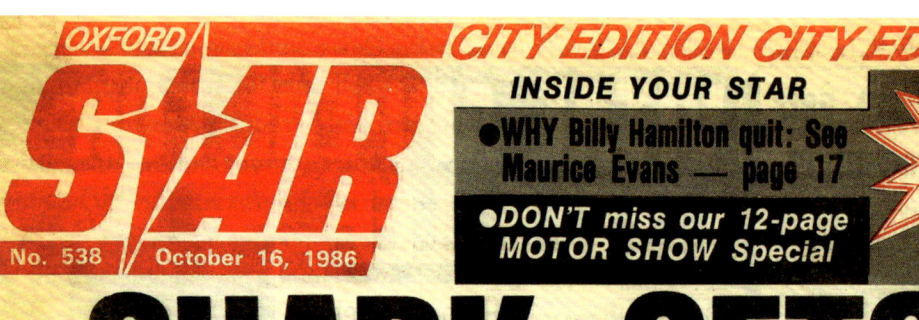

OXFORD
ST★R
CITY EDITION CITY EDITION

INSIDE YOUR STAR
- WHY Billy Hamilton quit: See Maurice Evans — page 17
- DON'T miss our 12-page MOTOR SHOW Special

Super 72 pages

No. 538   October 16, 1986

SHARK GETS SIX MONTHS

By KERRA LOCKHART

TO THE disgust of many local residents, Headington's controversial rooftop shark has been given a temporary reprieve.

Oxford city council's planning committee decided yesterday that the shark is an illegal development and must ultimately come down.

However, their decision is not to be enforced for six months so that art and shark lovers can pay last respects to the fibreglass fish that spectacularly plunges through the New High Street roof of cinema owner Bill Heine.

Mr Heine, who had the 25ft sculpture erected this summer as a personal statement against nuclear war, insists that shark as art is outside the jurisdiction of planning legislation and vows to appeal against any enforcement notice to the Department of the Environment.

"Through this decision to destroy the shark they are using the planning laws to limit artistic creativity," Mr Heine said after hearing of the council's decision.

The shark has become one of Oxford's top tourist attractions and put suburban Headington on the world map. The pros and cons of that attraction clearly divided councillors on Wednesday, as they debated what, if anything, could be done about the sculpture.

Labour's Alan Griffiths gave an impassioned speech in defence of both

Rooftop jaws wins a short reprieve

sharks and artistic freedom.

"The very fact that it has provoked debate indicates the shark is a success. It has entertainment value," Mr Griffiths said.

"I think Mr Heine has been pulling our leg very successfully and I move we allow him to get on with it," he added.

"That's the most irresponsible contribution to a debate I've heard in a long time," retorted Mr Griffith's Labour colleague, John Power.

Mr Power argued that the shark was nothing but a publicity stunt by Mr Heine to promote his two cinemas. "Let's be absolutely frank about this. The man is a nutcase. A nutcase," Mr Power continued.

Many of the councillors feared that if the shark stayed marooned on the Headington skyline it would create a dangerous loophole in planning laws.

"This has all been fun while it lasted but what

next? Is the shark going to have a family?" enquired Conservative John Stanyer.

Before deciding to issue a delayed enforcement notice against the shark, the planning committee was given a summary of 21 letters of support for the shark and 32 objections. One neighbour described the shark as vulgar, in bad taste and conflict with the character of New High Street.

★Bill Heine's plummeting piece of 'art'

ENDANGERED SPECIES !

THE HEADINGTON SHARK

THE RECENT GALES MAY NOT HAVE DISLODGED THE HEADINGTON SHARK, BUT CITY BUREAUCRATS, BEHIND CLOSED DOORS, HAVE HATCHED PLANS TO DO SO.

The Court has ruled that Sharks on rooftops require planning permission and Mr Bill Heine, the sculpture's owner has complied with this edict. Meanwhile the Shark hunters in City Hall have pre-empted the coming Planning Committee meeting, by deciding, without public consultation, that the Shark must go. !   This meeting is scheduled for early March and action is required NOW.

The Shark has many friends; if you are one, you can help save this Oxford landmark. Make you views known in writing, or telephone;

The Shark is the inspiration of two men, Mr Bill Heine and sculptor John Buckley. It was conceived at the time the Americans bombed Tripoli via the UK and erected on Nagasaki Day 1986. For further information contact: S.O.S Committee, 21 New High St, Headington, Oxford.

Printed by Bartset Press. Recycled paper by

A.J.Walker Esq,
City Planning Officer,
Clarendon House,
52 Cornmarket Street,
Oxford OX1 3HD.
Telephone Oxford 252183.

News of the temporary reprieve hits the local headline.
Courtesy of the Oxford Mail/Oxford Times (Newsquest Oxfordshire)

It's a small, but startlingly bold step. The Arts Council is putting its head above the parapet during a lull in this political battle and declaring its support for a Shark condemned to death. At the end of the grace period if I refuse to take the Shark down, the £1,000 will have gone to support an illegal object. If the Shark is ripped out of my roof by Oxford City Council, the £1,000 will have gone to a work of art that has been officially trashed.

The Arts Council at this very early stage breaks every bureaucratic safety rule and takes a huge risk of being pilloried by the press in giving the Shark's tale a leg up. Reaction is swift. This editorial appears in the *Oxford Times*:

> *'Why on earth should the Arts Council give a grant of £1,000 to the man who created Headington's famous (or infamous) Shark-in-the-roof sculpture? What is happening to our sense of accountability over public money? One constantly hears of genuinely needy organisations being denied money by the Arts Council – local theatres, for instance – yet here is a substantial sum handed over to what at best is a highly contentious cause. Although Oxford City Council has served an enforcement notice against the Shark's insertion in the rooftop on planning grounds, there are some members and some citizens who regard it all as faintly amusing. It isn't.*
>
> *To claim architectural merit for it is about as ludicrous as the action of the Arts Council itself. This is a case where the planners are right, mostly because it is not difficult to foresee what could happen to a city centre like Oxford's if such disregard for good planning was to go unchallenged. There do have to be some limits.'*

This award flushes the enemies out from the bushes. Now we know where the sentiments of the local press really lie. At least this shows the mindset of the editorial team.

The Arts Council support throws up views from some unlikely quarters as well. The Reverend Graham Midgley is from the village of South Hinksey adjoining Oxford, and he doesn't pull any punches.

> *'The Shark itself is not a work of art. Its likeness could be reproduced – and possibly is – in many a fair and pleasure beach. But it is the excitement, shock and fun of seeing this creature plunging through a roof in a respectable, lower bourgeois row of houses, which lifts the heart and gives a passer-by a jolt and a "something strange" experience which, heaven knows, we need in this hum-drum grey world.*

Artist John Buckley's view of councillors agonising over art.

What can we do to support Heine in his fight against the deadening Philistine forces of flattened-out mediocrity? Perhaps it could be possible for the Shark to pierce the roof of that monstrous lump of pseudo-renaissance stonework where our Lord Mayor and Council pontificate on art?'

The subject of art in Oxford touches several nerves dealing with good taste, humiliation, dignity and even love. But I have no idea how deep the sense of revulsion for the Shark can run. Patricia Weeks from West Oxfordshire describes herself 'as a lover of Oxford':

'I would like to support those people who wish to see the Shark, that ludicrous object, removed from the roof of 2 New High Street, and dignity restored to this ancient fringe of the City. There are some who are impotent to do anything about it, are even nervously trying to look on it as a form of "modern art".

Recently I stood behind a tittering group who had strolled to New High Street to view the object, and the general opinion seemed to be that it was a right giggle. I felt deeply ashamed and angry. After all, what is there now to stop anybody erecting a monstrosity above their property if they have a mind to do so, regardless of the humiliation caused to other people with a modicum of good taste? I am aware that this is somewhat emotional in tone, but I make no apology for this. I love my home city, and grieve over what is being done in and around it, either for lack of good taste or a sense of beauty or from lack of love.'

Chris Mullineux, a professional planner, comes by to inspect the Shark and thinks it will enhance New High Street.

'What does Mr Heine achieve by his patronage of John Buckley and by making his house available to display a work of art for public enjoyment?

Overnight he is doing something that millions of words of legislation, advice, commentary, case history and research have been unable to do. He is making planners stop and think. The profession has become bureaucratic, mundane and boring, having lost the sparkle which it had during earlier decades of rebuilding, growth and relative financial security.

If it does nothing else, the Shark promotes intelligent thought and stimulates discussion about planning, about art, about tourism, about fish, about building structures, and, above all, about the ordinariness of much of our environment.'

The Arts Council award encourages even artist John Buckley to join the fray:

'I am the sculptor who created this piece of art. It was put up on the anniversary of the bombing of Nagasaki, August 9, 1986; and it speaks of our vulnerability: "the house" invaded by foreign objects, "the house" ringing of all our worst nightmares.

When I first started work on this sculpture I wanted to reflect the underlying fears and anxieties of our society using a ready-made object – "the house", bricks, slates, window boxes, lace curtains . . . and one of our most feared and mysterious beasts, the Shark. I am an artist who has tried to reach more people than only the "art world" and its specialist audience. I make sculpture for public places, and I deliberately set out to create a piece of art that would provoke thought, laughter, argument and pleasure. I can't see it coming down for years. Too many people like it.'

Of course just because you have public support on your side doesn't mean you will win the battle. You still have to find out where the real levers of power are and engage them. A £1,000 award by the Arts Council and thousands of signatures on petitions from supporters are straws in the wind. Or perhaps, in this storm that is swirling around I'm just clutching.

SOS – Save our Shark

The Shark now has a new status (thanks to the Arts Council) that penetrates the thick doors of 'City Hall', and as a result during a meeting of the Oxford City Council Planning Committee almost one year after the sculpture first nose-dived into my roof the members take a new view.

Alan Griffiths, the Labour Leader of the council, heads the move to save the Shark and argues that local residents who initially opposed it have now changed their minds. 'People have come to learn to live with the Shark, and have come to love the Shark. This sculpture, from being something eccentric which people got cross about, is now something residents take pride in. It's put New High Street on the map.'

One resident, Mrs June Whitehouse who lives on the opposite side of the street, is so ardent about it she's named her house 'Shark View' and here's why: 'I'm dead against the Shark being taken down. It's world famous and unique. I've lived in this street for more than twenty years and the Shark has really brightened up the area.'

The Labour Leader warns that if the Council insists on ripping the Shark from the roof it will make the members look 'obstinate and bureaucratic' and he even calls me 'a major public benefactor'. In an impassioned speech, he then reads out other letters of support for the Shark, shows its picture in brochures on Oxford and points out the official support of a £1,000 grant from the Arts Council. He says it is clear that the public approves of the sculpture and asks its opponents: 'Why are you supporting the views of a minority who want to tear down something that gives enormous pleasure to the people of Oxford?'

Mrs June Whitehouse names her house 'Shark View'.

He urges councillors to vote for freedom, humour, imagination and common sense and to lift the harpoon from the Shark. These comments are rebuffed by an angry Labour colleague, John Power, who says the Shark is a 'monstrosity' and he labels me a 'crazy anarchist'.

'There is no evidence', he goes on 'that people have changed their minds about it.' Mr Power is on his feet charging around the room like a latter-day Captain Ahab, determined to drive a stake through the heart of the Shark. But his fury turns to apoplexy when he finds he has almost no support at the table. The blood vessels on his face stand to attention in a serious salute to shock, disbelief and disgust.

The pro-Shark faction wins the day, and in a vote of 7-2 the planners change their minds and decide the big fish is swimming on course for a permanent reprieve.

The Defender of the Faith in the Shark (Alan Griffiths) defends the outcome: 'It would have been absurd for us to take any action that would result in ripping down a work of art which has been recognised by the Arts Council. I would have been disappointed if it had been torn out of the roof and I think people of Oxford would have been too. It is a victory for common sense – and good humour and tolerance.'

A remarkable U-turn certainly; but it all hinges on another full meeting of Oxford City Council to approve this in two weeks.

An editorial in the *Oxford Mail* points out the U-turn is also an apocalyptic turn: 'The essence of the matter is that the city council over-reacted in the first place. If it had not been so committed in its opposition to the Shark its U-turn would not now be so noticeable. Nevertheless, if they give in to Sharks sticking out of roofs the whole of the Oxford skyline could theoretically be changed by works of art carrying the blessing of the city council.'

The enemies of the Shark go into overdrive and crank out another petition 'to

The Shark divides opinion as Oxford City Council play the 'precedent' card and the fear that every rooftop could potentially have a Shark on it, as captured by this Jim McClure cartoon (right). While the council seem intent on hooking the Shark off the roof, popular support in favour of it continues to build up (below).

Courtesy of the Oxford Mail/Oxford Times (Newsquest Oxfordshire)

SIGNS OF THE TIMES

PRECISELY WHAT I MOST FEARED, FORTESCUE — THE SETTING OF A PRECEDENT...

OXFORD STAR

CITY EDIT

No. 576 | July 16, 1987

FIN-TASTIC!

Shark is set to stay — by popular demand

OXFORD'S famous shark could become a permanent part of the skyline of the City of Dreaming Spires.

City councillors yesterday did a U-turn and gave cinema owner Bill Heine's big fish a huge vote of confidence.

A delighted Bill told the Star: "The shark has devoured all its opposition. I don't often praise the city council, but their decision is a victory for the shark and common sense."

The city's planning committee voted 7-2 yesterday NOT to go ahead with an enforcement order to tear down the rooftop shark.

Time was running out for the shark as the order was due to expire at the end of this month. Councillors originally objected to it saying it breached planning regulations.

RESPECT

Bill was drawing up plans to appeal, but yesterday's decision was "a vote of confidence in the shark," he declared.

"It shows that the councillors have taken public opinion into account. The people of Oxford have come to love and respect

By ROY COOPER

the shark as an important piece of art," he said.

The full city council will meet later this month to discuss the shark, but it is expected that they will back the planning committee's change of heart.

Council leader Alan Griffiths was behind the move to reprieve the shark.

Coun Griffiths said after the meeting: "I am pleased the committee made its decision to give the shark an indefinite stay of execution.

"It would have been absurd for us to take any action to destroy and pull

Public hooked on landmark

★ HEINE: Delighted   ★ GRIFFITHS: Reprieve

down a work of art which has been recognised by the Arts Council.

"I have always been a great defender of the shark and I have the strong impression that the climate of opinion in the Headington area was very much moved in favour of it.

"I would have been disappointed if I had been torn out of the roof and I think people of Oxford would

have been too.

"It is a victory for common sense — and good humour and tolerance."

Earlier this year the Southern Arts Council awarded the shark's creator, John Buckley of Wallingford, a £1,000 award for his memorable skyline sculpture.

POWER

Bill erected the shark in his roof in New High Street, Headington, last August — making headlines all over the world — as a statement "about CND, nuclear power, Chernobyl and Nagasaki."

At first neighbours were horrified by the 25ft high glass fibre sculpture, but it has since become a major tourist attraction.

★ Saved: Oxford's roof top shark

reiterate our continued and total opposition to this Shark. Let there be an end once and for all to this tasteless joke.'

They list all the old arguments:

- ◤ **Life is Hell** – 'The influx of sightseers has not slackened one bit.'
- ◤ **House Prices Plummet** – 'The Shark is a public nuisance which lowers the value of property in the street.'
- ◤ **Shark is a Killer** – 'Someone will get maimed or killed in an accident because the Shark is a distraction.'

But the petition has two new attacks on the Shark based on proximity and precedent. The Council 'should pay greatest heed to the opinions of those most affected by the structure . . . It is notable that certain members of the street who are in support of the structure live far enough away not to suffer the consequences of its presence. As an example, we would cite here the occupant of the rather inaptly named house "Shark View" from which the Shark cannot be seen at all!'

But the real big new gun in this debate is based on proliferation and precedent.

'The Council must be aware that if it permits the structure to remain, it is setting a dangerous precedent whereby any structure, outlandish or otherwise, may be built onto houses without planning permission by people claiming it is a work of art.'

Finally the petition argues that 'the City pay for the transfer of the structure to a place more suited for its viewing. We would suggest the new swimming complex in Cowley.'

This is novel and probably the first time anyone suggests that Sharks and swimmers are a recipe for success, but it does strike a chord with local pensioner Hilda Hitchcock: 'Mr Heine seems to think he is a benefactor to mankind. Instead of which he is indulging in his own childish whims. Put the Shark in a swimming pool.'

With the ammunition of 49 signatures on their petition the residents walk into the next full meeting of Oxford City Council. It could be a bloody battle, but it isn't. Councillors ignore the elephant in the room, like film buffs talking about camera angles, the use of colour and the soundtrack, and not mentioning the meaning . . . anything but the meaning.

Yes, we hear about house prices. The Shark has not devalued property in the street. According to local estate agents, over the last six months house prices have risen in England by 4.5%. In Oxford house prices have gone up by 7% but in New High Street the cost of a home has soared by 12%. Estate agents even use the Shark as a selling point and advertise local homes as having 'excellent views of the Shark' and describe property as 'located in the world-famous New High Street, home of the notorious "Headington Shark" '.

And no, the Shark is not a killer. There has not been one accident in the street because of cars slowing down to view the Shark.

Yes, the Shark can be seen from 'Shark View'. Its owner reveals that 'unfortunately for us there is a "close season" for Shark viewing when the lilac tree at 13 New High Street is in flower and full leaf! Of course we can still see the Shark from the gate and part of the front garden. As for the consequences of the Shark's presence, those which I experience are the joy of meeting and talking to the people who come from many parts of the world to look at and photograph the Shark.'

The bottom line is that the Councillors are out of their depth. They don't know what to do. The Shark has outfoxed them. Then tempers begin to fray. John Power, recently promoted to Vice-Chair of the Planning Committee, is fed up after a year spent discussing the pros and cons of the Shark and wants it down – 'now!':

'It's absolutely offensive that the Planning Committee of this city can even consider allowing the Shark to stay. What Bill Heine has done is an insult to rate-payers of this town. Other people who want to make outside structural alterations to their premises have to abide by the law and submit planning applications and the appropriate fee for the work.'

John Power persuades the full council to reject the Planning Committee's recommendation to rescind the enforcement notice that would kill off the Shark. 'If we consulted about the enforcement notice, in natural justice we should re-consult before taking it away.'

Mr John Power backs people power. He wants to find out what local residents really feel about their now world-famous tourist attraction and he dismisses my petition signed by 101 people who live in the Shark Street and want it to remain. 'Anyone can whip up support. Let's face it, this town is full of esoteric idiots who will sign anything.'

Fire and Water

The Shark is kicked around by bureaucrats, wrapped in red tape and left to die between Committees in the treacherous shallows of Local Government.

The Planning Committee members change their minds and say the rooftop Shark must come down, but at the same time they also decide to find the Shark a new home in Oxford 'to preserve its artistic merits', a tactic which gives me the one weapon I need – more time.

I drop a hint to the Councillors about how successful their new ploy will be. 'You have missed the whole point of the Shark. The power comes from it crashing through the roof disturbing the family living inside. It cannot be separated from the house.' They don't get it because the full council by a narrow margin of 22 : 18 supports this re-housing policy. But where do you put a homeless 25-foot Shark?

The sculpture is passed on to the Recreation Committee which controls access to all the swimming pools and arts centres in Oxford. After three months, the Recreation Committee report says the Shark 'should ideally be located on another roof top, otherwise it will lose its impact as an anti-nuclear war statement, but most roof tops in Oxford are not structurally designed to accommodate Sharks'. The report rules out swimming-pool roofs on visual grounds because people would object to having a Shark as a neighbour. They have also inspected the interiors of all pools and refuse to put the Shark inside since that would require structural alterations.

They leave no stone unturned. 'The parks and recreation grounds in Oxford should remain a Shark-free zone because the international notoriety of the Shark will attract vandals and souvenir hunters.'

One committee member Lynne Lawrence has a novel suggestion. Why doesn't the City Council re-create a play Shark which looks exactly like the one in the roof and put this in a park for children to play on? They agree to instruct council officers to examine the idea and calculate the cost of constructing a Shark playground toy. But some councillors are concerned about whether toddlers could get hurt by this play Shark and they want to know how much it would cost if every neighbourhood wanted one, which they think is highly likely.

After one year the Councillors finally agree to move the Shark to the Old Fire Station Arts Centre in Gloucester Green close to the centre of Oxford. City Architects make several drawings to show how the Shark would look on the roof and in the foyer.

Councillors choose the lobby 'particularly because we do not need planning permission for it'.

A belt-and-braces approach wins the day; even though they don't need permission they intend to ask themselves for it. Then councillors go the extra mile and send their recommendation to the Finance Committee with a request that the City Council pay for planning permission.

The full council collectively jumps for joy at this final resolution of the Shark problem and votes overwhelmingly to move the Shark from the roof of my house to the lobby of the Arts Centre. Tory councillor Ann Spokes still supports the roof site and pens a poem during the debate. . .

The city want the Shark to hide
So they suggest it go inside

But the Shark and house are one
That is why it is such fun
A Shark without its roof on high
As work of art would surely die
A Shark with nose stuck in the floor
Would not delight us any more.

I'm impressed by the generosity of the councillors to use public money to pay for re-locating the sculpture:

> *'I am sure all artists in the area will be delighted that the council wants to put up more sculptures in the town. Although you have a good site it is by no means the perfect site for this sculpture. The house and the Shark are one complete work of art – the hole in the roof created by the Shark is as important as the rest of the sculpture. I am amazed that councillors completely miss this.'*

Courtesy of the Oxford Mail/
Oxford Times
(Newsquest Oxfordshire)

The press and the public don't miss it. An *Oxford Times* cartoon invades the council debating chamber.

The 'Letters to the Editor' page throws up this question – 'Does Oxford City Council actually have the legal power to take any resident's property, or work of art, say, and put it where the City Council chooses without the owner's consent? This is a frightening prospect for people living in Oxford.

My local Conservative councillor Major General Tom Gibson rushes into print with a reply:

> *'A Work of Art? Those of us who view such things in a different light, perhaps regarding them as the work of charlatans, are entitled to our viewpoint; and we are supported by planning regulations!*
>
> *If memory serves aright, citizens have been compelled to demolish entire storeys, to remove additions and to change designs in cases where planning permission has not been sought, or regulations flouted.*
>
> *This particular monstrosity was installed without permission. Council has decided that it must go, subject to the condition imposed by council members determined to protect the perpetrator of this hoax.*

Let one of these councillors, most of whom live comfortably far from the thing, demonstrate the courage of conviction by applying for planning permission for installation on their own property. Failing which, let them withdraw their protection and consign the thing to that most suitable of all possible sites, the Redbridge Rubbish Tip!'

His view is suspect, according to one Oxford resident, Stella Waterman:

'I question the motives behind Oxford Council's decision to re-locate Oxford's Shark house sculpture to a more suitable position and ask "why?" The fact that the structure was erected on the anniversary of the bombing of Nagasaki to emphasise man's vulnerability is not only an extremely powerful statement in itself, but also particularly relevant to our situation today. Is the council devoid of all artistic sensitivity? Had Mr Buckley, as creator, not thought the present location – a small terraced house, similar to millions throughout the country – to be exactly right to form part of his sculpture, he would not have put it there in the first place.

It is a powerful piece of sculpture which I have come to enjoy and I do not agree that it should be re-located. I protest – and I am not alone.'

She certainly isn't. One pillar of the establishment, a local vicar writes: 'How did the citizens of a great city like Oxford manage to elect such a bunch of unimaginative, legalistic, small-minded Gumbies? Contrary to planning regulations, indeed!!! What is the point of suggesting that another site should be found "to see if it could be preserved as a work of art"? What ignorant nonsense.'

Thomas Braun thinks the Shark is a hideous piece of spoof commercialism. 'But even if, like some of our councillors, I quite liked it, I would not for a moment advocate an abuse of our planning laws which makes any of my fellow-citizens' lives miserable. If this goes through, what won't, if it has enough money behind it?'

The Shark is about many things but not one of them is big money. The total cost so far is postage, photocopying and telephoning, well under £25.00. All materials, labour and advice have been donated. No one is throwing money at the Shark or buying its way past the Planners' nets. In financial terms this is a 'common or garden' Shark.

This debate doesn't even register with most of the elected Councillors. They are now above the fray because they have made a decision and they are marching forward, not listening any more to the voters. 'Contrary to the impression the Council appears to be seeking to project,' writes Shark supporter Patrick Reynolds, 'I understand that many of the more sensitive local residents – and this is, in any case, not simply a local

Sculptor John Buckley captures the raw emotions of the debate in Oxford City Council when the Shark comes up on the agenda.

matter – positively welcome the presence of the Shark. As for the protesters, they should get down on their knees and thank Heine for putting a bit of zap into their boring little street.'

The councillors are so determined to march forward they don't realise I am not in step. It takes councillors a whole year to discover that. The Planning Committee finally sends the Shark back to full council with a recommendation to attack. 'No progress has been made about an alternative location within the Old Fire Station and an indefinite delay could prejudice a prosecution.'

This is familiar territory. As an editorial in the *Oxford Times* points out, I've been here before:

> *'The continuing case of the Great Shark Controversy ("This will run and run" – remember?) provides as congenial an example of Local Government at Work as one could wish for. The Planning Committee's Shark-fishing enforcement order was originally confirmed by the full council, albeit with due delay to allow wet-suited council officers to explore alternative waters for the beast. Well, having completed their explorations, the officers prudently consigned the problem to the Arts and Recreation Committee (who else!), who have nevertheless now returned it to the Planning Committee (naturally): who will, no doubt, return it to the Solomons of the full council again. And – always supposing a decision then results – why, has not the Shark's proud owner promised that he will appeal to the Secretary of State, or Caesar or someone? Thus do the wheels of local government turn. But we do not wish to knock the system; the way things are, we must be grateful for any light relief it can produce.'*

Light relief? These people aren't playing softball. They have issued an Enforcement Notice that orders me to remove the Shark and re-instate the hole (not my roof). I address the full council in tones that are ringing, if not respectful:

> *'Hello. It's good to see you again. It's always good to see you individually: one by one you're wonderful. It's just when you all get together in a group that I have my doubts about you. Normally I would give you the benefit of the doubt because I'm prepared to overlook certain quibbles, lapses and mistakes. In fact I'm prepared to overlook almost anything except nonsense; and that's the only way to describe your Enforcement Notice.*
>
> *You are requiring me to take two steps. First remove the fibreglass Shark from the roof of my house. Second, reinstate the hole made to accommodate the Shark in the roof. The first step is clear, but the second is far from clear*

because it requires me to reinstate the hole in my roof, not to reinstate the tiles on my roof. How does one reinstate a hole? Do I make it larger, wider, deeper or smaller? Presumably if you have something sticking out of the hole, in this case a Shark, then you have to remove the object so you are left with only the hole. This way you have re-instated the hole, put it back to its original function as a hole without a Shark in it. So are you ordering me to remove the Shark from the roof and leave the hole?

This "notice" is written with Alice in Wonderland language. How can anyone be forced by the local authority to have a hole in the roof? And if you take this case to court on the basis of this current Enforcement Notice, the case will be thrown out on a technicality.

So I'm here on two counts. I'm here to defend the Shark and to fight the Council in Court. I want to win, but I don't want to win on a technicality. I was rather hoping this fight could be a serious match. I don't want to get into the ring and find my opponent is a bungling bantamweight.

In the second place I'm a taxpayer and I do not want to see public money wasted by the Council on a misguided legal adventure. No matter how much Lewis Carroll might have enjoyed all this, I'm not sure your voters will find it very funny.

If you do want to pursue the hunting of the Shark, make sure your weapons are accurate and come up with an Enforcement Notice that has some teeth, not like this current piece of nonsense. When you get your act together I'd be delighted to see you in court; until then, good day.'

They respond with cheers and jeers.

When I try to leave the chamber, City Council solicitors are blocking the door and thrust an envelope into my hands. I open it later to discover they have served me with a summons for trial in the Magistrates' Court for failure to remove the Shark.

Oxford City Council's deliberations on the Shark attract national media attention, as with this feature in the *Sunday Correspondent* (now defunct) by Francis Wheen.

Bill Heine did not apply for planning per[mission] before installing a 25-foot shark on the ro[of of his] terraced house. Three years later, Oxford [Council] is still trying to bring it down. BY FRANCIS [WHEEN]

Left, Bill Heine and his fibre-glass shark on the roof of his terraced house in Headington, Oxford; *below*, the 25-foot great white shark appears to have fallen from the sky and nose-dived through the roof of 2 New High Street: in fact it is held in place by steel girders; *below right*, the shark has now become a tourist attraction to rival the dreaming spires.

O[ne] fine Saturday [in] August 1986, a [great] white shark [crashed] through the ro[of of] Heine's terrace[d house,] 2 New High Stre[et, in the] Oxford suburb of [Heading]ton. The effect was breathtaking. Some passers-by giggle[d], gawped. The postman was so startled that he dropped [a few let]ters before racing home to fetch his wife and children.

Heine, a local cinema-owner, beamed with pleasure [at the] success of the operation. He had prepared his house by in[serting] steel girders and joists in his attic, ready to support four hun[dred] weight of fibre-glass shark. The model had been transp[orted] under cover of darkness from the chicken shed outside O[xford] where it had been built by local sculptor John Buckley. The[n, while] Heine's neighbours in New High Street were settling down [to] their breakfasts, the monster of the deep was winched up o[n a] huge crane and lowered nose-first into the specially prepared he[ole] in Heine's roof. And there it was left, tail and fins pointi[ng] heavenwards, roof-tiles scattered around it, as if it had ju[st] dropped out of a clear blue sky.

The court case ratchets up the pressure on me a bit but sends out massive shock signals to some supporters, in particular students at Oxford University. An officer of the Junior Common Room at St Anne's College wants to help by making the Shark an honorary member. Postgraduates in the Middle Common Room of Hertford College go one step further: they write asking me to consider Hertford as a new home for the Shark.

> *'Hertford has a history of supporting change and innovation in Oxford. The Shark, for us, represents the same progressive spirit. It symbolises the importance of challenging convention. . . . As part of our bid to bring the Shark to Hertford, we have circulated a petition in both the Middle and Junior Common Rooms. It has met with widespread support.*
>
> *Few Oxford colleges make any sculpture available to their students or visitors, certainly nothing on the scale of the Shark or with the same contemporary feeling. Having the Shark itself in Hertford would redress this imbalance, and draw art out of the museum and into the public eye.*
>
> *In addition, the relocation of the Shark to Hertford would preserve the prominence it has gained in Headington. We are concerned that unsuitable locations may be proposed by the City Council, locations that treat the Shark as a joke or an aesthetic "one-liner".'*

It is an attractive idea and with a court case looming, perhaps I should be developing 'Plan B'. This would allow the Shark to live on and have the energy and power it has in my roof, much better than the Council's timid and tiny-minded approach of shoving the sculpture inside an Arts Centre lobby. John Buckley, the sculptor, visits Hertford College, takes some measurements and produces a drawing of the Shark plunging through the historic Bridge of Sighs (*see opposite*).

The students are delighted and prepare a planning application to put the Shark in the Bridge; but the vice-chairman of the Planning Committee, John Power, dismisses the idea: 'The Bridge of Sighs is in a Conservation Area. It would not even be considered because the object is to conserve the arch in the form it is now.' Mr Power added that even if the Council did grant planning permission, it was most unlikely that the Department of the Environment would give the necessary listed-building consent.

He then goes on to dismiss me: 'People in this town are sick and tired of the antics of this crazy Canadian nut-case.' He doesn't have that description quite right – I'm from the United States.

Maybe that 'American' aspect is one reason why the planners are so at sea with the Shark. They are used to dealing with people who know their place, who are so steeped in the rules they don't push the boundaries, so bound by procedure they don't ask questions. Perhaps it takes someone outside the system to challenge the system.

When rules should be broken

▲ The fact that the Shark broke the rules and was put up without permission is not something which should influence those making a planning decision about whether it should stay or go.

▲ If I had followed the rules and submitted a planning application before the Shark was erected, there is no doubt at all that permission would have been refused and any appeal would have been dismissed.

▲ It is only after the erection of such a bizarre structure that any rational assessment of its power, worth and impact could be conducted. What I did by erecting this Shark on my roof was to take this discussion about public art off the page and turn it into a three-dimensional event – a living thing that people can connect with, live with, think about and decide 'yes, it has value or no, it is rubbish'.

▲ So for something like the Shark to have a fair chance of survival in the crucible of public debate, it must first breach the big taboo and be born.

▲ In this case breaking the rules was logical, reasonable and fair.

And people are unlikely to take that step of breaking the rules if they are part of a system that rewards anyone for ticking the right boxes and not thinking outside those boxes.

The Bursar of Hertford College is probably part of the system. Dr James Bertie describes the Shark crashing through the Bridge of Sighs as 'nonsense'. He warns that the students would not only need planning permission from the local authority, but

also the consent of the college which owns the bridge and that would be unlikely.

Oxford's Chief Assistant Planner, Linda Wride, also pours cold water on the idea: 'The students may find that, when they have to pay a fee for their application, their idea doesn't actually materialise.' She likens the students' suggestion to plans in the 1970s to build a pyramid on Christ Church Meadow and put a giant sculpture of a cat on the Castle mound in central Oxford.

It looks like the students' Plan B is dead in the water, and this is welcomed by Stephen Lord from Eynsham on grounds of class warfare:

> 'I frequently travel through Headington by bus (as befits a member of the working class) and weary from my labour as I am, my spirits are raised by the sight of the Shark proudly defying the revisionism of the reactionary ruling classes.

> Tradition and continuity are essential facets of the British way of life and are not limited to the so-called upper class, and I view the thinly-veiled attempt by the Oxford University Establishment, through the offices of Hertford College students, to hijack "the people's Shark" with deep suspicion. Removal of the monument from the simple artisan's cottage and its subsequent implantation in the Bridge of Sighs at the heart of the University area would be a serious blow to the proletariat of this city.'

The *Oxford Times* and *Oxford Mail* pursue the story as it develops in the council's debates. Cartoonist Jim Needle captures the mood with his wry observations (top).
Courtesy of the Oxford Mail/Oxford Times (Newsquest Oxfordshire)

To June
from Matthew

Sharks in the street

In this public debate about the future of the Shark, the *Oxford Times* knows how to stir the pot. The editor runs an item in the leader column asking a simple question:

> *'Yes, we know you've heard the one about the Shark embedded in the roof of a house in New High Street, Headington, since August 1986. And this week, you'll have heard of city council plans to move the Shark to the lobby of the new Gloucester Green entrance to the revamped Old Fire Station Arts Centre (no planning permission required).*
>
> *The Shark's owner insists that "the Shark and the house become a work of art and to remove it from the roof means that the council wants to destroy the power of the Shark". What we have never understood is how the Shark, a creature of the deep, became airborne in the first place.'*

This strikes a chord with old and young alike. Roza Jeffery, aged 10, writes a poem – Three Questions:

Mummy, Mummy, Mummy,
Please tell me the truth,
Why has Mister Heine
Got a Shark stuck in his roof?

In his bedroom ceiling,
Has he got the head?
And does it give him nightmares
When he goes to bed?

Roza, if only you knew just what kind of nightmares and some of the creatures who slither around in them . . . And your question about the possible head in the bed reminds me of two films: *The Godfather* and *Taxi Driver* because one Oxford cabbie keeps telling his passengers that my wife is divorcing me since she can no longer stand to sleep in a bed with a Shark's head above it. The taxi driver spins a nice tale but no, Roza, there is no Shark's head. An early photograph taken by the sculptor John Buckley while creating the piece of art shows his son Ant crouching inside the Shark; and Ant's head is the only head (*see opposite if you don't believe me*).

The Shark connects with the fears of many children and Kate Mills puts her finger on this.

'I think your house is the most marvellous house ever made because of the Shark. When I was little I always thought that the head of the Shark went through the roof and was visible from the inside and it would also eat little children because it was so realistic. I am eight. Sincerely, Kate.'

George Malcolm, at the other end of this spectrum of life, is dying of cancer at Oxford's Sobell House Hospice. In his version, once again there is a monster lurking about:

Down in the South Pacific, mid
The equinoctial gales,
There lived a family of Sharks
Along with cod and whales.

Mister Shark and Missus Shark,
And Baby Shark, made three;
I must confess to everyone –
That Baby Shark was me!

My mum was quite a beauty,
But this really lovely dish,
Had to admit that my real Dad
Had been a flying fish!

When I learned that, I understood
Why I took great delight
In swimming to the surface, and
Then taking off in flight.

My little Shark friends, down below,
Would swim around and stare
At me whilst I was doing
Acrobatics in the air.

One day, at fifteen thousand feet,
(I couldn't fly much higher)
A great big thing whooshed by me with
Its fins and tail on fire.

Somehow, this thing caught hold of me
With such tremendous power,
It whisked me off behind it at
Six hundred miles an hour.

At London Airport, I came loose,
Shot on, above the Shires,
Until I started stalling
Over Oxford's gleaming spires.

With power gone, I nose-dived down
And ended my long flight –
I crashed into Bill Heine's roof
Where I am still stuck tight.

So, whilst Bill's version isn't true,
There's one thing I must say –
It's costing him a packet just
To feed me every day!

I'm now a great attraction, I
Draw tourists in for miles –
And I'll bet Oxford Council
Never caused so many smiles!

With apologies to Hans Andersen's *Little Mermaid*, June Whitehouse writes not about monsters, but about people who are unkind.

Your leader writer wondered how the Shark came airborne – he probably has never heard the story of the Little Shark . . . The Little Shark lived deep in the ocean and she was unhappy as she was taught in school that when she grew up she must eat smaller fish and even attack humans. One night the Little Shark crept from her sleeping place and went to the Shark Witch. "I want to be a friendly Shark", she wept. The Witch Shark told her that many humans were not friendly either but that in Oxford some people might come to love a Shark. The Little Shark shut her eyes, the witch spoke magic words and the Little Shark woke to find she was on dry land, and felt all floppy and peculiar. Standing over her was a kind man called John who comforted the Shark and moulded her into the right shape and she looked beautiful.

One morning at sunrise John said, "We are going to your real home today" – a pulley was put round her waist, she was lifted high into the sky. The pulley tickled and she felt rather sick. When she was gently lowered into her roof she realised she was part of a sculpture which could show people in this uncertain age that unless they lived together in peace their roofs, too, might be shattered.

The Shark remembered the words of the witch and found some of the humans were unkind, some even wanted to cut the sculpture in half, but many came to love the Shark and wanted her to stay.'

A London furniture maker argues that the spirit and sense of our times is revealed by the Shark.

'Human beings are deeply fascinated by the highly improbable. The sculpture hovers on the limits of credibility. Is it possible for a Shark to fall from the sky? One can almost say that such a thing could never happen, but I am left with a nagging suspicion that it could. It just might by a freak accident and it just might in a mysterious way and incomprehensible way. There is something about the times in which we live that induces us to believe such a possibility.'

Matthew, a child patient at the Oxford hospitals near the Shark, travels past my house regularly; and he catches the zeitgeist in his drawing called 'Sharks in the Street' about things lurking under the surface.

Three-year-old Amaya, daughter of my neighbour Andy Gordon, doesn't like the story that a man built a Shark in the roof of his house. 'She prefers to hear that the Shark would see the birds flying over her head as she swam around the ocean. She really wanted to join them, so she flapped her fins with all her strength and took to the skies. But somewhere over Oxford she remembered fish can't fly, and came crashing down into the house in Headington, where she now lives eating beans on toast. The moral of the story: keep believing.'

I walk into the Magistrates' Court with my eyes wide open. I know this is a risk. The stakes are high – this could be the end of the Shark. This could also be very expensive and the end of me. But the rebel keeps believing.

The prosecution by Oxford City Council is designed to extend its powers at the expense of the individual's. But I welcome it so we can clarify the law and discover if there is a small ledge of freedom left where artists and architects can begin to brighten the dull, conforming environment which so many people in England resent. A frightening thought is that maybe the Council do represent the majority wanting a world which is safe and featureless?

My solicitor, Eric Church, tells the Magistrates that I am seeking to argue in the High Court that Oxford City Council's enforcement order is null and void because the Council does not have the power to order the removal of the Shark. The sculpture is an art form, not a 'development' to be judged by planners. 'It would be quite wrong for this court to proceed with the case in the knowledge that an application is going to be made to the High Court.'

The Magistrates agree and give me four weeks to apply to the High Court. I get to know my solicitor well in this short span. It is like the bond between two mountain climbers who are also bound by a rope; they have to understand the person at the other end of their rope very well – and possibly very quickly.

Eric has misgivings about the case. We have two arguments: a technical one – the Council has not served me with all documents of the Enforcement Notice thereby disadvantaging me; and a defence on a point of law – a work of art does not need planning permission. Eric thinks the Court is not the proper place to make the defence that art works are exempt. I should have done that earlier in an appeal against the enforcement notice. We are on shaky ground.

On the appointed morning, Eric and I walk together down St Aldate's to Oxford Crown Court for the first criminal trial of my life. Eric is in high spirits and drops this nugget into the conversation. 'I've been practising law for almost a half century. I'm getting on in life and I don't defend criminals any more.'

I wasn't prepared to let that one go – 'Why not?' 'Nowadays' he says, 'criminals just aren't what they used to be.' I'm strangely comforted and consider that a compliment.

It is a bad day in court.

My barrister argues that the Enforcement Notice ordering removal of the Shark is invalid because it is not accompanied by the usual documents advising me of my right to appeal. The judge, Peter Crawford QC, dismisses this and rules that the validity of the Enforcement Notice is unaffected whether or not it is delivered with other documents.

Judge Crawford goes on to dismiss the defence that the Shark is a work of art.

'This court has no views whatsoever on the aesthetic merits or demerits of this object . . . planning permission has not been granted.'

Under these rulings I have no option but to change my plea to guilty.

Then he puts the boot in.

'You have flouted the law in disobeying Oxford City Council's legitimate order to take down the sculpture and reinstate the roof.' [Hole, m'lord, hole, not roof!] 'You took the law into your own hands. You may think it is a bit of a joke and you may be right. But if people play jokes on the public and then persist it can become rather expensive.'

The judge says he had been intending to fine me a 'very substantial amount' but had changed his mind when he heard the likely size of the legal bills over the case. 'I fine you £1,000.'

There was more bad news. The judge ordered me to pay the costs of the council who claimed £4,635. I asked for an independent assessment. My solicitor, Eric Church consoles me:

'True to form, the City Council turned up at the hearing before the Judge with another wad of papers which had not previously been seen. Their claim for costs on this occasion had increased to £6,186.35. The Judge spent some time dealing with the question of costs, but in the end took a fairly rough and ready approach and ordered that you pay £5,000 for the prosecution costs . . . This is very unfortunate indeed. However, I still regard the prosecution costs as grossly inflated and it was correct to take a stand on the question of principle, but unfortunately this in the end has cost you money.'

There is one ray of light; the judge agrees to allow me to pay off the fine at £75.00 per week.

I hear no cheers at this outcome: but D. A. Stanhope from the village of Eynsham writes in my defence to the *Oxford Mail*:

> *'Can it be true that the City Council is seriously contemplating spending its electors' money on an act of destruction which will make it notorious around the world? Bill Heine's Shark, that fishy intruder from the heavens which has delighted so many visitors to Oxford, has achieved fame as a flash of imagination and wit. It has illuminated an age in which the visual*

Artist John Buckley's view of the legal rituals in court.

Application to the High Court.

environment reflects all too clearly the domination of our environment design by short-term, balance sheet considerations.

Instead of pillorying this patron of the arts, the council should be conferring the Freedom of the City on a man who has been prepared to expend his private funds on a public work of real aesthetic significance.'

Dave Headey from Faringdon also lends his support in a letter to the Editor of the *Oxford Courier*:

'I notice that while schools, factories and houses, for which presumably planning permission was granted, had their roofs ripped off in the storms two weeks ago, the Headington Shark stayed put.

I, for one, would be willing to purchase for a modest sum a copy of the plans for installing a Shark on a roof so that I can submit them to my District Council, and thereby (a) help Bill Heine to pay his fine and (b) demonstrate in a small way my feelings towards the faceless, humourless authorities who make the rules and do their best to stifle every idea that does not conform to them. I am sure there are enough of us who feel the same way in Oxfordshire alone to enable Bill to pay off the fine and donate the surplus to a charity of his choice.'

That is the question – How am I going to pay £6,000, even by instalments of £75.00 per week? I make an initial payment of £1,000 to start to clear the fine and some months later I give the court a lump sum of £675.00 and make arrangements with my bank to pay the remaining amount by direct debit.

A court official responds succinctly. 'I do not accept payment by Bank Credit Transfer into my bank account. I require payments to be made at my office.'

I hear my options closing behind me like a series of doors on a prison landing, so I write back to accept this quirky demand, and at the same time I go down the only other route available. 'I enclose 57 cheques at £75.00 dated for each week in which you require the payment to be received in your office and one cheque for £50 dated for the last week as the final payment.'

This is not acceptable to the Court either and I receive this little letter: 'At the time of conviction in respect of (the fine) you were committed to prison for thirty days, suspended on payment of £75.00 per week. You have failed to pay as directed by the court and the warrant committing you to prison now falls due to be issued.'

But an unlikely and accommodating gesture does come via officialdom when I receive a hand written postcard notice from PC 2872, Jake Smith, notifying me of a warrant for my arrest. It seems to get the measure of the moment with phrasing that might be taken as possible intent of sly support along the lines of 'I've got to arrest you, so pop by at your convenience'. I pay the whole fine immediately with a little help from my friends.

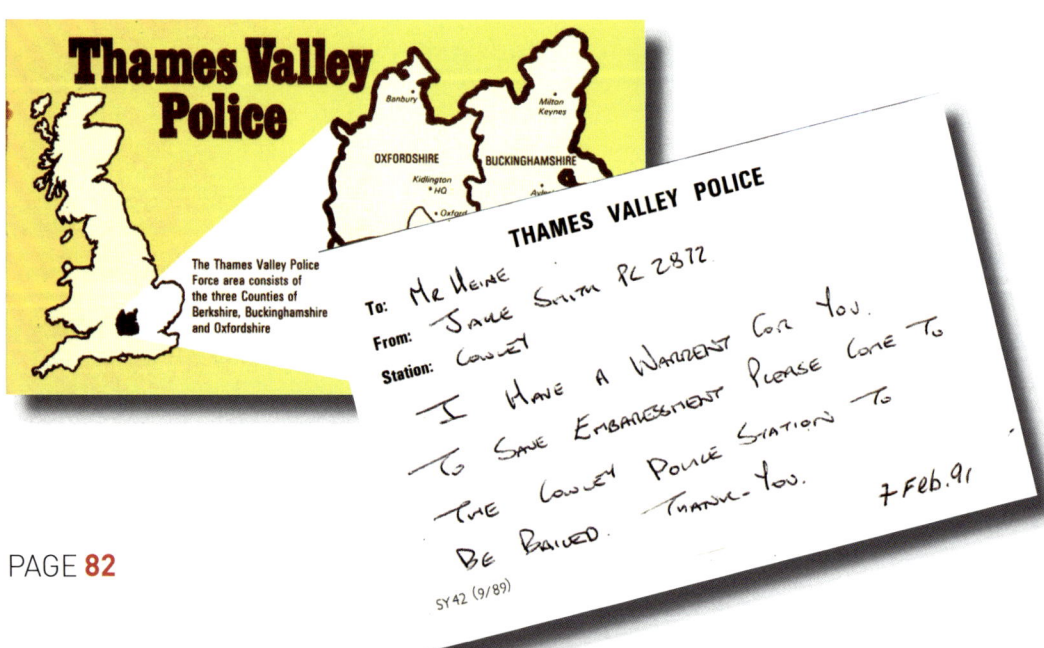

But where does that leave the Shark? Will it come down? I see people hanging around the house like vultures wanting to get one last look and take the last snap with their Kodaks. They think it's all over. I keep believing.

When you don't know where to go, go back to the beginning; and in the beginning four years ago Oxford City Council wanted me to submit a planning application. Why not? As columnist Reg Little of the *Oxford Times* reports – 'The nightmare of the Shark affair having to go through the whole planning process is certain to strike terror in the hearts of many councillors . . . just when Oxford City Council planners thought it was safe to go back into the committee room, the horror has returned.'

Defenders vs demolishers

I write to all members of Oxford City Council that many people in the Headington area and in the City and County now refer to it as 'Our Shark'.

'The sculptor, John Buckley, and I have in essence offered people this piece of public art as a gift, and they have graciously accepted it. I would like to think the City Council would be able to accept our gift with the same sort of grace, and I'm prepared to give them a second chance.

From the start I have argued, and will continue to argue, that public sculpture does not need planning permission – the planning laws were not set up to give local politicians a veto power over public art, to decide what images are appropriate or inappropriate for people to see. Members of the public are quite capable of making up their own minds in the matter.'

I take a conciliatory tone.

'In spite of these arguments, I believe there are still a few members of the City Council who would like the opportunity to discuss the piece of public art as a planning matter, and I have no objection to this exercise, however unnecessary it may be, and accordingly I enclose a planning application.'

Within two weeks the Planning Committee meets in secret session, with Councillor John Power now installed as the new chairman. Members instruct the Oxford City Council solicitor to start work on a further prosecution against me.

According to a report in the *Oxford Mail*:

'The City's Planning Committee decided to forcibly remove the sculpture from Bill Heine's house in Headington. Mr Heine will be ordered

to demolish the sculpture himself – but, if he fails, council workers will finish off the fish. This comes a month before the committee is due to hear a planning application from Mr Heine ruling for permission to keep his 25-foot Shark. Despite going ahead with plans to tear down the sculpture, the committee agreed to hear Mr Heine's application to "appear fair".'

From Leighton Buzzard the grandmother of seven-year-old Justin Roff writes to Oxford City Councillors accusing them of being far from fair. Justin is a severe haemophiliac and has regular treatment at the nearby Nuffield Orthopaedic Centre in Headington: 'The Shark has given Justin hours of pleasure because most of the time he is confined to a wheelchair and after his treatment he is allowed to go for a walk, just to see the Shark. How heartless of the Council to deny a handicapped child this small pleasure in his life . . . for the Council to say they will demolish it is unthinkable.'

The behind-closed-doors report gets a strong reaction from artist Roger Perkins of Old Boars Hill in Oxford:

> *The subject you are discussing is public knowledge and in large part positively supported. Why, therefore, hide relevant information and decisions from the public? This is not, I believe, democracy in action. If your committee was already aware of the forthcoming planning application before the 'secret session' it is surely a grave mistake to prejudge the outcome before hearing the application.*
>
> *I can only surmise that given the weight of favourable local, national and international opinion towards the sculpture that your committee seems bent on carrying out an act of municipal vandalism.'*

Two weeks later the new head of the Planning Committee, John Power, tells the press the Council would not forcibly rip out the Shark, but that I could land in court again if the Council refuses planning permission; and Mr Power goes so far as to speculate on the kind of judgement and sentence I might get by saying a judge could impose daily fines for failure to remove the Shark. The *Oxford Times* article finishes with this observation: 'Mr Heine has now applied for retrospective planning permission for the fish, but that is likely to be refused by the Planning Committee next week.'

Encouraged by the victory in Court and the comments of the judge and empowered by a new chairman who openly supports the hunting of the Shark, members of the committee are in no mood to compromise. They sense the tenor of the times and all the official signals are saying 'go for the kill'. What I don't get is where this deep-seated desire to destroy the Shark comes from. What has unleashed this fury against the Shark when there is so much support for the sculpture?

Nancy Rudden from North Oxford writes to the editor of the *Oxford Mail* and touches on this question:

'I am sad to read that council workers may be ordered to tear down the Headington Shark. I have often seen it and think that while not every home should have one, this piece of sculpture is well done, striking and humorous. It has become a tourist attraction and as its fame has spread so has the amused amazement at the critics who keep seeking its removal.

Perhaps Mr Heine is an irritant and so becomes a target for the type of people who bolster their personalities by attacking a person or group. Would that such vehement energy be used to deal with real problems! There must be a list of repairs waiting for the attention of council workmen but it's always easier to break down than build up and usually more fun. Rooftop Sharks should not proliferate like garden gnomes. But why not let this solitary specimen remain? Follies of past centuries are now preserved and even restored, valued as interesting eccentricities.'

The *Oxford Times* runs an article shortly before the Planning Committee meeting under the title 'Shark Popular with Public':

'The public has given Bill Heine's rooftop Shark an overwhelming vote of approval. A substantial majority expressed support for the sculpture in a consultation exercise staged by Oxford City Council.

The Council received sixty-one letters and three petitions in favour with seventeen letters and one petition against. The outcome is a major fillip to Mr Heine's fight with the Council to retain the Shark on top of his house.

The Council is steadfastly opposed and has already agreed a strategy to get the Shark removed.

Petitioner Martin Jennings declared: 'We regard it as an Oxford landmark and a valuable work of art.' A second petition demanded to know: 'Is the Council blindly attempting to apply the regulations at all costs?'

But it is no great surprise to find the Planning Committee votes to refuse permission for the sculpture. If the full council decides to accept this recommendation, it's curtains. We are now in the 'sudden death' section of the game.

This is a tricky time, and certainly not a time to get involved in another debate, especially one as explosive and divisive as the Thatcher government's new local community Poll

With my solicitor, Eric Church, and the Shark becomes a Poll Tax payer (above).

Tax which is at the centre of demonstrations and riots around the country.

And yet that is precisely what lands in my letterbox – a Poll Tax demand payable immediately addressed to Mr Great White Shark, 2 New High Street, Headington, Oxford. The council also sends a letter advising the Shark of how it might appeal against this charge. 'You may feel that you are exempt and should not be on the register.'

This sparks a public debate in the press and A. Bouzid from Yarnton writes: 'Oxford City Council have at last acknowledged Mr Great White Shark as a member of our community, affected by the Poll Tax. I would like to advise Mr Bill Heine, who stated that Mr Great White Shark "would be applying for maximum relief", not to forget that he should at least be able to get Mr Shark an immobility allowance.

I personally have never seen Mr Shark anywhere but in his strategic and fixed roof position in New High Street. An immobility allowance is no doubt good grounds for tax relief in this case.'

Mrs Daphne Greenaway from the village of Churchill has definite ideas on this:
'How stupid can people get? There are many people like me who do not think that the Poll Tax is a joke. We are just worried how we are going to pay it. That Shark has wasted too much of the ratepayers' money already.'

A spokesman for Oxford City Council says that someone had sent in a form registering the Great White Shark as a Poll Tax payer and it had been entered on the official register. He agrees that the form I received was sent by the council but the entry has now been deleted. I'm delighted.

The full council hunkers down into two camps over this death-penalty debate – the killers and the connivers. The dividing line doesn't have so much to do with age as attitude; some people are up for an adventure, others want their cup of cocoa, an early night and no demands.

I open the debate with the claim that the Shark is one of the most important pieces of public art in Britain since the Second World War. The Councillors don't dispute that; they just ignore it.

Then I mention the Germans . . . again. I know that the City Councillors have received from Bavaria a petition entitled 'Save our Shark' with 55 names, addresses and professions, which states: 'We have seen the TV report about the Shark done by John Buckley, and we all think it is a gorgeous idea which is worth to keep.' The councillors aren't impressed.

I bring out the survey of local people in the Shark Street – yes, I tell them, that's how it's known – where I contacted 151 people from a total of 83 houses in the street: 149 signed the petition in favour of the Shark. I've searched the letters and petitions in the planning office over the last three months and report that according to the Council's own files 85% of people in New High Street support the Shark. I can see a bit of a twinkle in some Councillors' eyes.

Irene Williams from the Alison Clay House sheltered accommodation opposes the Shark because it is an eyesore, has no planning permission and draws groups of tourists. I've never understood her argument which boils down to the claim that a great many people go to visit an eyesore. If the Shark were an unattractive, ugly blot on the landscape, it would not attract the number of tourists that she says come to see it.

She also warns the politicians 'If this goes through there will be no control over such things as satellite dishes on roofs.' That idea of control frames the debate. Councillor John Power argues that if the application for the Shark were approved it would weaken planning control in Oxford.

Labour member Peter Moss takes up the argument. 'I am confident that a majority of the Council has now grown very fond of the Shark. If I had the choice I would rather have a thousand Sharks around Oxford's roofs than one single, horrible satellite dish.'

The traffic problem surfaces in an article in the *Oxford Mail* before the Council meeting:

> *The notorious Headington Shark is rivalling Oxford's dreaming spires as a tourist magnet. But Oxford's most famous fish may be on its way out. New*

city bus firm Spires and Shires has re-routed some of its tourist trips to take in the famous Oxford landmark. Director Ceri Fielding said: "It is a big tourist attraction and it is gaining nationwide fame. We thought it should be included because it is so unusual. When the bus pulls round the corner into the street all their jaws drop. It certainly gets them talking.""

Ceri refutes claims that the Shark attracts hordes of tourists who cause congestion.
    'As a company we specialise in small, off-the-beaten-track, tours of Oxfordshire. We therefore pass or stop at the Shark with a maximum group of 14 people on some of our tours . . . we specifically do so because it is an interesting curiosity on a relatively traffic-free street.'

And Ceri hands the councillors a petition of 31 signatures from visitors of 12 countries as far away as Singapore, Australia and New Zealand: 'Having visited the Headington Shark, we would like to voice support for its continued existence on the grounds that it is a unique and rightly renowned folly and work of art.'

In a lively debate one Councillor asks whether it was going to remain 'a lone Shark'.

Labour member Christine Simm suggests that 'Councillors here should listen to the people who elected them and allow Oxford's popular Shark to remain.'

Tory Councillor Ann Spokes ends her speech with a plea: 'I do hope this Council will see sense and not bring itself into ridicule. This is a beautiful and artistic creature which should be allowed to stay on her roof.'

I am not sure how the vote will turn out. It is tense and so am I.

Perhaps it would be better to admit defeat now and walk away with whatever dignity I can salvage from this. There is a part of me that says 'enough and no more'. I've fought but maybe it's finished. After four years the Shark's tail is still telling a story from my roof. Does it need to continue? Haven't I made the point? And anyway what is the point now?

I started out by asking the question – how safe are we from the decisions by people in power? If I take down the Shark because people in power force me to, that in itself is an answer to the question; so even defeat will be a kind of victory. I'm braced for the bad news.

It's a knife-edge vote – 21 to 20: the pro-Shark faction wins the day and hands the condemned Shark a last-minute reprieve.

There is a slight silence while councillors absorb the shock and then the flood-gates open to let out the laughter and anger, the relief and horror. Some politicians on both sides sit still and are very quiet. The look in their eyes tells you they are not ready to believe it yet.

A lot of people are simply stunned.

I know this isn't success yet. The Planning Committee still has to grant approval, but the full council has backed the Shark for the first time. It catches me on the hop. Where do we go from here?

'Your ridiculous and offensive erection'

One place I do not expect to go is Margaret Thatcher's Lions' Den where the big beasts of her political jungle debate the Tory Party Manifesto for the next general election. But the Shark is dragging me there.

I get a single-sentence note from John Bright, my boss at BBC Radio Oxford: 'It disturbs me that your ridiculous and offensive erection should have resulted in yet more pressure being applied to that nice Mr Baker.' He also encloses an article from *The Times* entitled 'Plea for Unauthorised Building to be a Crime'.

Kenneth Baker is the chairman of the Conservative Party and the first target of a new campaign to change planning laws and make it a criminal offence to build without planning permission. The force behind this drive is the District Planning Officers Society – yes, when they all get together that's what they call themselves. They want a high-profile person like Kenneth Baker to come on side and champion their cause.

These people know how to run a campaign and they've done their homework. There is growing concern about an unauthorised gypsy site near Kenneth Baker's home in his constituency in the Mole Valley. The Society argues that people like these gypsies who deliberately flout planning laws for profit or self-interest must be stopped. Present controls on development are inadequate, ineffective and too slow.

As a prime example of what is wrong with the current planning system the District Planning Officers Society points the finger not only at the gypsies, but also at me: 'The campaign is being launched after a spate of infringements of planning laws, including the case of the "Headington Shark" at Oxford, in which William Heine was fined £1,000 at Oxford Crown Court for refusing to remove a twenty-five foot glass fibre Shark from the roof of his house.'

At the very time when sculptor John Buckley and I are asking for more freedom to be creative locally in Oxford, the national body of planners is trying to restrict that area of freedom and close down the debate nationally for the whole country and deter others by creating a criminal sledgehammer to crack this nut.

If their campaign is successful they will hit us with a double whammy: We will have a national Conservative government with a policy to kill off things like the Shark

increased traffic in New High Street by 18%. If you were looking at a house bringing 18% more traffic into a street you would feel very strongly about it.'

In reply Councillor Nonny Tiffany argues – 'The increase in traffic is really very, very small. If you have a work of art in your area that is something people will want to see, it's something you have to put up with.'

The chairman, John Power, leads the opposition to the Shark:

> *'We have spent public money over four years resisting this application. We have ignored consistent advice from our planning and legal officers. We have ignored those who live nearest the Shark who oppose it, and we have ignored the views of the three ward councillors who also oppose it. We have to have a consistent approach to roof-top development. If we approve this I want to know what we are going to do about other roof-top developments on this agenda. Will we recommend the applicants go ahead with their plans without permission, and how will we deal with it if they do?'*

Councillor Ann Spokes answers. 'Where a work of art is proposed, that will also be considered on its own merits.'

The committee does not capitulate to the spirit of uniformity and votes 7–5 again in favour of keeping the Shark.

As a spectator in this quite English equivalent of a bull-fight, how do I deal with the un-English desire to kiss some of the councillors?

Plan of attack

In the run-up to the full council meeting passions run high. I receive yet more petitions and poems and the 'letters to the editor' column in the *Oxford Mail* keeps the debate on the boil. Patrick Gray, until recently a member of Oxford City Council, writes with conviction:

> *'I think the Council should give planning permission for the Shark without further delay – as it should have done four years ago when the issue first arose. I note the opinion given in Council by the previous Chair of the Planning Committee, Albert Ramsay, that: "There are no adequate planning grounds for refusing permission". . .*
>
> *'The full council has now rejected the proposal that permission be refused and the Planning Committee voted in favour of giving it. Yet the minority who are opposed continue to find new and ever more far-fetched ways to prevent permission being granted.*

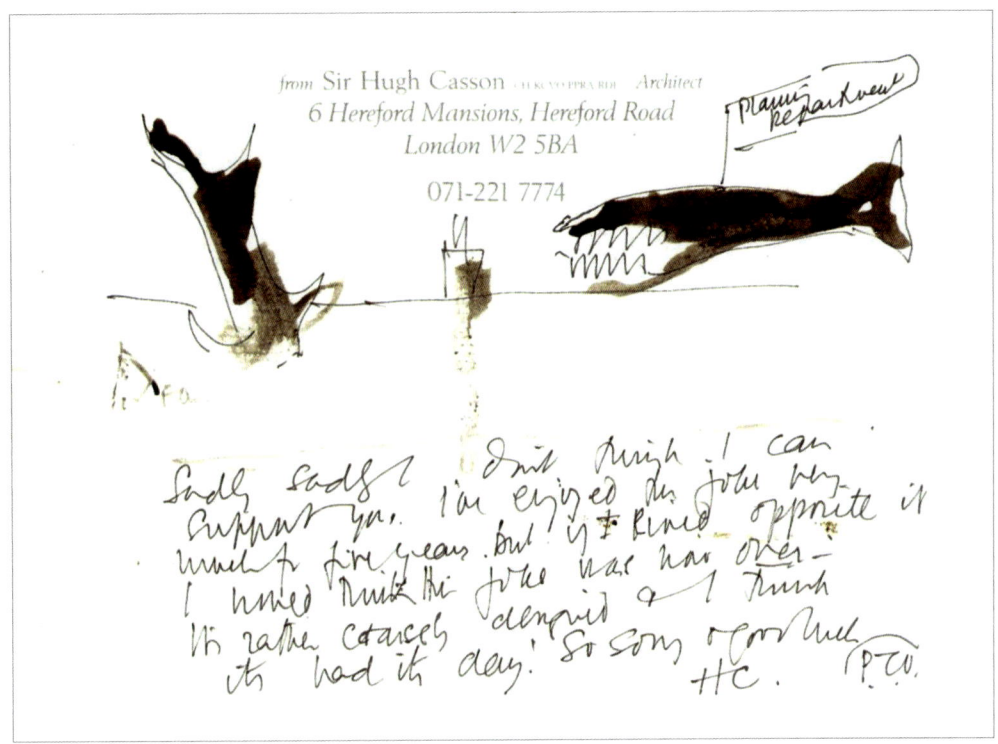

from Sir Hugh Casson *Architect*
6 Hereford Mansions, Hereford Road
London W2 5BA

071-221 7774

The note from Sir Hugh Casson translates as: 'Sadly, sadly, I don't think I can support you. I've enjoyed this joke very much for five years, but if I lived opposite it I would think the joke was now over. It's rather coarsely designed and I think it's had its day. So sorry and good luck, HC (PTO) Also as a priggish architect I think buildings, however modest, deserve their share of dignity, No?

Over the years, some fairly extraordinary arguments have been put forward against granting planning permission. We have been warned that if Mr Heine is allowed to put a Shark on his roof "everyone will do it". History has proved this fear ill-grounded. . . We have even been told, believe it or not, that the only proper place for a Shark would be in a children's swimming pool!

All the evidence supports the view that it is overwhelmingly popular with Oxford residents – including those living nearby. It is a curious *irony that a Council which is committed by its own recreation strategy to supporting the popularisation of the arts should be trying to force the removal of one of the very few genuinely popular pieces of sculpture in the country. I have followed this issue closely since the beginning. I am convinced, I am sorry to say, that opposition to the granting of planning permission has had very little to do with planning consideration and a lot to do with Mr Heine's failure to treat the council and councillors quite as seriously as some would like. . . I believe very strongly that planning applications should be determined on the basis of planning considerations and the wishes of the public.'*

Laurence Harwood who has for years organised opposition to the Shark takes exception to Patrick Gray's claim that the Shark is 'overwhelmingly popular with Oxford residents including those living nearby':

'He is culpably wrong and seems to be working on the principle that if a story is told often enough it eventually becomes true. Is he unaware of the opposition of the people living around the structure or does he just conveniently choose to forget it?

The truth is that opposition by the forty local residents who live in an almost unbroken ring around the Shark continues. It is our view that must be taken into account – not that of signatories of one of the many petitions that Mr Heine so loves to collect from shoppers, tourists and passers-by. . .

Sticking twenty feet or so above the skyline it is much more intrusive [than a loft conversion]. Loft extensions are not floodlit at night but Hr. Heine is fond of doing this with the structure. The Shark is also apparently different to a shed or a shop sign, as applications for planning permission for these in New High Street failed in both instances. In the case of the shop sign, this was on the grounds that it would be too intrusive!'

The debate in Council is fiery and rakes over old coals but one novel tack comes from the leader of the Conservative group, Janet Todd, who claims that 'Mr Heine has bought the house just to put the Shark in it. Houses are meant to be lived in not to put Sharks on.'

Pro-Shark supporters accuse the opponents of being 'blimpish' and of attempting to punish Heine for cocking a snook at the Council'. But anti-Shark councillors argue that planning regulations had to be obeyed and it would be irresponsible of the Council not to enforce them.

The money argument raises its head when John Power warns that the Council would lay itself open to a charge of wasting public funds on the court procedure if councillors now change their minds. Of course I had to pay the court costs so there was no expense to the Council, but no one picks up on this and the argument is not challenged.

When the debate ends the tension is tremendous. Councillors do not vote in the usual way by a show of hands, but by the Lord Mayor calling each name out and publicly recording the vote. It goes down to the wire with the full council voting by a majority of just one to send the application back to the Planning Committee for its members to 'think again'. The Shark loses by a Nose.

It's back to the planners: Before the next Planning Committee meeting, the former chairman of that committee and Shark supporter Albert Ramsay comes up to me and explains that a close friend of his has died and the funeral is today and he really could not miss the ceremony. He explains that he thinks this will make no difference to the vote on the Shark because he expects that will happen well before he has to leave and he still intends to vote to keep the Shark.

If members may have to leave in the middle of a meeting for an exceptional reason such as a funeral, it is common courtesy to advise the chairman of this possibility, just as he is telling me as a matter of courtesy. I keep one eye on my watch and the other on proceedings. The chairman John Power takes several items on the agenda before the Shark and the debates do seem to stretch out rather slowly and proceed at a snail's pace.

At the appointed hour of the funeral, Albert Ramsay bows out of the meeting and leaves. Shortly afterwards the chairman brings up the subject of the Shark and quickly says that the decision on whether it should stay or go has already been taken by the full council. He tries to move on to the next item. This causes a bit of an uproar and several councillors protest that they have had no opportunity to question whether the decision taken at full council should be binding or should be the last decision.

Councillor Barbara Gatehouse says 'I think that we can bounce this back and forth *ad infinitum*' and she proposes a motion to refuse planning permission for the Shark.

Without the support of Albert Ramsay, the vote is split evenly – five to five. There is some uncertainty and a moment's hesitation while the chairman John Power announces that in this situation of a tie vote he, as chairman, is allowed a second vote to break the tie. The final motion to kill off the Shark is carried on the casting vote of Mr Power.

PART THREE

THE PLANNERS STRIKE BACK

DATELINE: 20TH-21ST JUNE, 1991 – CURRENT

Linda Wride leads the Oxford City Council team at the
Public Inquiry, taking a somewhat ambiguous position as
this moment by John Buckley captures – notice the fingers
crossed on her hand behind her back (above).

Planning permission denied: Oxford City Council Planning Committee has used its knock-out punch and I'm hanging from the ropes, but they still they take a pop or two at me. I appeal against the committee's decision to refuse planning permission for the Shark and request a Public Inquiry. This doesn't go down very well and the chairman decides to hear a confidential report on the future of the Shark during a secret meeting when the press and public are excluded.

<big>13</big>

SHARK SHENANIGANS

This 'confidential' report is leaked all over the press. One article in the *Oxford Mail* with the headline 'Council Chiefs put the Bite on Shark' makes lurid reading. 'The Headington Shark faces a new threat from council chiefs. They may order workmen to forcibly remove the Shark.' The report says that since I lost the court case last year for failing to obey a five-year-old council order to remove the Shark from the house and reinstate the hole, 'failure to obey the notice after the conviction is a further offence – with the possibility of an unlimited fine'.

Another article entitled 'Shark could be Taken by Force' actually quotes the 'confidential' report which says that Oxford City Council has the option to rip out the Shark and charge me for the damage this would do to my house. This isn't the first time the planners have raised the spectre of a dawn raid with chainsaws to remove the Shark and probably isn't the last time they will put the frighteners on.

I request permission to address the committee. The officials say they have never had a request from the public to address members on a confidential item. One possible reason for this historical fact is that the public is always kept in the dark about items on the 'secret' agenda. But here they have leaked it in a spectacular manner.

They refuse my request to address the secret meeting because I'm not supposed to know anything about the confidential items. Where is Lewis Carroll when you need him?

But then things begin to look up: I read another article in the *Oxford Star*, under the heading 'A Fishy Inquiry for Bill, but will Poll Tax payers have to pick up the tab for the hearing?' The Secretary of State for the Environment announces that he will definitely go ahead and hold a Public Inquiry into the desirability or otherwise of the Shark crashing into the roof of my house. The article provokes a menacing reaction.

'Oxford City Planning Committee Chairman John Power, on hearing that Bill's request for an inquiry had finally been granted, recalls that the inquiry into British Rail's planning development of Oxford's station car park site two years ago cost £75,000. But we are now allowed to claim costs from the other side provided we show that we've acted reasonably. And we definitely shall in this case – if we win.'

Is this the council rightfully flexing its muscles or sending a signal that I should drop the appeal, take my punishment before it gets any worse and limp away with my tail between my legs?

The article then quotes a council spokesman: 'Technically we have the right to go in and forcibly remove the Shark, and send the bill for the work to Bill. But it is this council's policy to wait until all avenues of appeal are exhausted, including an inquiry.'

In the movie *Butch Cassidy and the Sundance Kid* the outlaws are pursued with relentless vigour by a posse over the rough terrain. Finally the two men are holed up on top of a mountain cliff with nowhere to go but take a death-defying leap into the river five hundred feet below. Sundance spies the posse in the distance charging straight for them with rifles raised. He turns to Butch Cassidy and says 'Who *are* those guys?' I'm beginning to understand what he means.

Mentioned in dispatches

In the run up to the Public Inquiry several people write me saying they think I am very courageous (read foolish) and offer their sympathy about how much this is going to cost me! But isn't it wonderful that I'm prepared to put my neck on the chop for my beliefs? Obviously they know nothing about what drives a rebel to the bitter end. And this 'end' may well be bitter because we have lost virtually every round in this fight so far. The Public Inquiry is the last throw of the dice and like gambling, this one is an addiction too. Nobody tells me I'm not supposed to win. I still believe I can. Bring it on!

Both supporters and opponents of the Shark write to the Inspector of the Inquiry and I receive a copy of each letter via my solicitor, Eric Church. According to him the split is about 95% in favour and 5% against – which sounds a bit too good to be true. I scrutinize each letter. The writers are aware that they are players in a potentially bloody bash and don't hold back their punches . . . on both sides. And some are heavyweights.

The Chairman of the Arts Council of Great Britain, Lord Palumbo takes a strong stand: 'The sculpture has now been in place for some time and has received tremendous popular acclaim. It is an extremely compelling image and it has been featured in magazines and newspapers throughout the world, creating great interest and, not least, attracting many visitors. What is otherwise an undistinguished part of Oxford is redeemed by this remarkable sculpture and, in my view, it would be a tragedy to lose it and a grave mistake on the part of Oxford City Council to deny planning permission.'

In defence of Headington, Councillor Turner (who lives there) describes Lord Palumbo as a 'crashing snob' and claims the sculpture turns New High Street into a 'small scale Disneyland'.

Oxford-based author Philip Pullman is

'strongly in favour of the Shark, and of Mr Heine's right to put it up and keep it there. I would be just as firm in my attitude if he lived in this road and put it up next door to my house.

I think it's a splendid object. It is beautiful, it's surprising, it's funny, it's poetic: it cheers me up whenever I go past it. It is quite obviously a work of art, and one which is unique to Oxford. No other city that I know of has anything like it. We've got a wealth of antiquity here, beautiful old buildings by the score, but we're not so well off for contemporary art that we can afford to destroy this wonderful fish. It's a witty, strong, and beautiful piece. If it goes, Oxford will be committing an aesthetic blunder on the scale of a crime.'

Some people like Mary Madens of Headington are fighting for the dignity of the City of Oxford. 'It is a hideous monstrosity that should never have been allowed to be displayed on the roof of his house. Oxford is a City of great beauty, and Oxonians are very proud to live here. We are *not* pleased that a total stranger should be allowed to make this particular area a laughing stock.'

Mrs Joy Custance is succinct. 'I beg you to order the removal of the roof-top Shark in Oxford. It is a monstrous eye-sore, a ridiculous vanity and an insult to a great City like Oxford.' And Maurice Waterhouse urges the Inspector

'to rid Oxford of this ugly absurdity . . . it inflicts a hideous blot on the scene by its sheer size and vivid representation of a shark's catastrophic death, by crashing headlong from above into the roof of 2 New High Street, implying a very painful and bloody death in the attic.'

Local landscape consultant Hal Moggridge, member of the Royal Fine Art Commission 1988-99, disagrees:

'This piece has become an identifying mark for the City of Oxford worldwide. I have heard Oxford referred to by a Japanese colleague in South America as "the City of the magic Shark beside the University of dreaming spires".'

And Maire Brankin is also concerned about Oxford. 'As a resident and trader in this beautiful historic City, I write in support of keeping "the Shark" in her present

ARTS COUNCIL

14 Great Peter Street
London SW1P 3NQ

071-333 0100

FROM THE CHAIRMAN

23 September 1991

The Rt. Hon. Michael Heseltine MP
Secretary of State for the Environment
Department of the Environment
2 Marsham Street
London SW1P 3EB

Dear Mr Heseltine,

I am writing in support of the planning appeal for the retention of the shark sculpture ("Untitled 1986") at 2 New High Street, Headington, Oxford.

The sculpture has now been in place for some time and has received tremendous popular acclaim. It is an extremely compelling image and it has been featured in magazines and newspapers throughout the world, creating great interest and, not least, attracting many visitors.

What is otherwise an undistinguished part of Oxford is redeemed by this remarkable sculpture and, in my view, it would be a tragedy to lose it and a grave mistake on the part of Oxford City Council to deny planning permission.

Yours sincerely,

Palumbo

Lord Palumbo

from Lord Esher

Christmas Common Tower, Watlington, Oxford OX9 5HL

telephone 049.161.2604

20 Sept. '91

Dear Secretary of State

APP/G3110/A/91/184337

I write as a former President of the RIBA & Rector of the Royal College of Art to support the above Appeal.

This is one of the very few truly popular pieces of public sculpture in this country, I think because it is striking, amusing and enlarges the imagination. It is the only visually interesting feature in an architecturally benighted part of Oxford, and I am sure there would be widespread sadness if it were to be removed.

Yours sincerely

Esher

RECEIVED 23 SEP 1991 11/17

Pressure mounts on the Secretary of State for the Environment.

position. The Shark embodies spontaneity of achievement and humour in art in a City which is in danger of being "set in aspic". It is laudable to preserve our heritage but part of our heritage is the present. I believe that "the Shark" is a serious work of art. Please allow her to continue to wave her tail joyously.'

John and Christine Taylor think the Shark may bring something other than joy. 'My wife and I are absolutely opposed to allowing the so-called "Roof top Shark" to remain. It would be a permanent incitement to all sorts of *anarchy*. The rule of law is our only protection.'

Architect Derek Stanhope looks at the legal framework from a different perspective:

'The Shark delights many and offends others. What the Inspector has to assess is if this is a major artistic happening whether we as a society ought not to make room for it. Our laws and regulations are made for the benefit of the community as a whole. We would diminish ourselves, I believe, if we become trapped by our own protective system. A test of wisdom is the capacity to perceive when in particular circumstances we have outgrown the rules we have devised. Oxford has received a lot of unflattering comment for its treatment of the City's fabric. For example this year vandals destroyed a public sculpture in St Giles. It would be tragic if we found ourselves having to explain to an incredulous world an act of state ordained vandalism.'

The Shark has become something more than a sculpture, for many it is a symbol of deeply held values.

To Scilla Elworthy, the Shark 'conveys a serious message about how unexpectedly we could be subject to the consequences of our lifestyle, and it makes people laugh as well – a very powerful combination. Please see that it is not removed.'

Paul Ingram thinks 'she has come to hold for many a symbolism of Man's inability to totally divorce himself from Nature. In times of great uncertainty over how we interact with our environment, and what the consequences will be of the relationship, this serves as a timely reminder.'

'The Shark is an important public monument in Oxford,' writes John Hamwee.

'It is amusing but it also communicates a serious message: that in this time of unparalleled interference with the natural world, unlikely disasters are to be expected. It is this combination, I think, that has made it internationally famous and certainly many visitors regard it as an important part of seeing Oxford. It would be not just a great pity, but an act of contemporary barbarism, to remove a much loved and much respected work of art from this city.'

Tei Williams argues that the

'Shark stands for a fundamental belief in this country that man should have freedom of speech, that man should be able to voice his ideals, beliefs, preferences, desires, needs and choices so long as they do not harm others in any way. This Shark in no way causes offence. I have taken much pleasure in walking along New High Street showing foreign guests the wonder of the freedom of expression that this country allows. I hope that I can continue to feel that pride in my country. Let the Shark remain.'

A lecturer at the Oxford College of Further Education, Jacqueline Worswick, is arranging a course for foreign students entitled 'British Institutions' about:

'aspects of British life which, to my mind, make Britain what it is. One such aspect is the admirable tradition of protest, statement, demonstration (call it what you will!) which in England has in the past taken very personal and individual forms. Your Shark sculpture and the reasons you had it erected where and when you did seems to me to be a perfect example of this.

I have been immensely cheered by the Shark, particularly in the present climate in Britain of, I feel, increasing intolerance of anything that is different, unconventional or, simply, artistic! I should love my foreign students to know that some of the aspects of British life and society which used to make me feel happy to be British are still alive.'

Several writers focus on the 'floodgates' and will the Shark inspire copycats?' Mrs S Tarzey thinks so: 'People who live there have to look at its decaying ugliness every day, and if it is allowed to stay after planning permission has already been refused, there will be nothing to stop like-minded exhibitionists from following suit.'

Former Lord Mayor of Oxford Olive Gibbs argues:

'Beauty, of course, is in the eye of the beholder and I have no doubt that there are worse sharks to live next door to than Bill Heine's fibre-glass exhibit at Headington, but if, without planning permission, the Shark is allowed to remain, is this not an open invitation for Bill's neighbours to have flying pigs, pink elephants and spotless leopards emerging from their chimneys?'

Most letter-writers mention this, including craftsman Martin Whitworth who asks the Inspector: 'Please allow the Shark to stay. We will not have sharks sprouting out of roofs all over the country but we will have something by which we can be stunned, and shaken out of our normal everyday terraced-street lives.'

Stephanie Jenkins rolls the debate into a crisp question.

'We are very proud to be neighbours of the Shark. You need not fear that the retention of the Shark will open the floodgates for a whole shoal of sharks – very few people have the money and chutzpah of Bill Heine. The Shark is unusual and stops people in their tracks; but it is not ugly or offensive. It blocks out no one's light and it gets in no one's way and is not advertising anything. So what's the problem?'

Oxford City Planning Committee comes in for a certain amount of criticism. Jack Yates, former county councillor and Mayor of the nearby town of Brackley, with his wife Mary 'consider that the Oxford City Council has taken a humourless and bigoted attitude to this affair which ill becomes the great City of Oxford. There is room in this increasingly gray and bureaucratic world for the unusual and eccentric. The Shark seems a harmless example of this. Those of us who do not live in Oxford find the Shark an amusing and by now quite famous symbol of what often seems a hopeless fight against mindless bureaucratic forces.'

David Huelin from Oxford also criticises the councillors.

'The Shark is not merely harmless; it is a work of art much admired by everybody except a few stuffy councillors who feel their authority has been flouted. The Shark lends a touch of originality to an otherwise very ordinary street, and it is clear that what is at the centre of the dispute is not the unquestionable aesthetic quality of the Shark but the amour propre of the Council. It is greatly to be hoped that the Secretary of State will strike a modest blow for originality and innocuous individuality against the dreary obfuscations of small-minded authority.'

Arts administrator Nicola Russell goes even further.

'I would like to register a protest against the protracted and senseless persecution of Bill Heine over the Shark in his roof. It is time to stop what amounts to petty harassment, and to leave residents and visitors alike to enjoy one of the delights of the City. So few people show any sign of initiative in this age of deadening bureaucracy – please do not allow this spark of creative energy and enthusiasm to be snuffed out.'

News Editor Brian Deacon writes that he is

'suspicious of the motives of some Oxford Councillors in their refusal of planning permission. I suspect the answer lies in the cloud of pomposity which seemed to hang over the Council chamber when this matter was debated. Mr Heine has not always stepped carefully in dealing with some councillors as deferentially as they would like. That, in my view, is why the full council over-turned both a decision of the planning committee to grant planning permission and the advice of officers.'

A fellow of St Edmund Hall at Oxford University says he thinks he's found the problem. 'For five years the Planning Committee and the owner and inspirer of the Shark have been at loggerheads, and throughout the controversy I have never read or heard a convincing argument from those opposed to it. I think that we have a severe case here of "Planners' Pique", a fury on the part of the planners that something was done without their consent, and something so spectacular that their rather limited minds find it hard to fit it into their way of thinking.'

Two Labour City councillors write to the Inspector in agreement. Bob Price says, 'I would like to put on record my support for the retention of the Shark public sculpture and my belief that the attitudes of Planning Committee and council members towards this planning application have been regrettably influenced by their dislike of Mr W. Heine's personal style and behaviour rather than an objective evaluation of the planning issues involved.'

Councillor Christine Simm echoes this view: 'I am afraid to say that a few influential councillors are determined that Bill Heine should be seen to be defeated on this issue for reasons that have little to do with the Shark as such.'

So what has been going on? What will this Planning Inquiry decide?

The answer to that question is absolutely nothing. Whether the Inspector grants planning permission for the Shark or orders its removal, his decision is about to be overruled. Exactly one week before the Inquiry begins I receive an unexpected letter informing me that due to the fact that 'the appeal relates to proposals giving rise to significant public controversy' the Secretary of State for the Environment, Cabinet Member Michael Heseltine, is calling this case in for his own personal decision.

The Public Inquiry still goes ahead, but since we all know the beady eyes of central Government in Whitehall are watching our every move, events take on an even more intense theatrical nature.

14

PUBLIC INQUIRY DAY 1: 'FRUSTRATION, FEAR AND FURY'

Legal teams from each side fight over the big differences of law and fact, but the small things make the most impact. Linda Wride, leading the Oxford City Council officers' team, wears a shark brooch on her dress the first day and on the second she uses a child's straw shaped in the form of a shark in her glass of water. Ms Wride gives evidence against the sculpture and when my legal team ask what her personal opinion of the Shark is, she declines to answer.

I give evidence as well and there is no question I won't answer. I let it all out, well nearly.

▶ *'The Shark appeared on 9th August 1986 and you may wonder why five years ago I ripped open my roof to put a Shark through it . . . what were my motives and what did I hope to achieve by this?*

The first house I bought was 2 New High Street. I took possession on 15th April 1986, the day bombs started dropping in Tripoli on houses that looked similar to mine in suburban streets. I remember celebrating early in the day at finally having a home of my own, and then later that night watching television pictures of explosives ripping through roof after roof of hapless houses. The day I became the owner of a secure, safe structure, I watched other dwellings destroyed, dwellings that their owners no doubt had also believed to be "safe as houses".

Later that month, 26th April, 1986, when the nuclear power station at Chernobyl erupted houses were again under attack. This time it wasn't bombs that left a trail of visual destruction, but radiation that came silently and swiftly to crash through the roof and invade suburban streets in Kiev. No longer could the owners of these "safe structures" close the doors and draw the curtains and keep the outside world at bay. No longer could each home owner be an isolated, invincible island. Now the houses and their inhabitants were all connected by a certain vulnerability and by the need to question how safe they were from decisions by people in positions of power.

There was a feeling among both friends and foes involved in these events – and we were all involved – a feeling of unease, of frustration, fear and fury that these things could have happened. There was apprehension that something similar might happen in comfortable leafy lanes. The unthinkable might take place once again . . . perhaps right before our eyes in our own street . . . in my house.

I wanted to explore some of the questions that incidents like these raised. I wanted to ask people to look at just how safe they were, how isolated, how connected to each other, and how much at risk from the threat of attack. I wanted to encourage people to look at their fears and their hopes and their bedroom slippers still sitting underneath the easy chair.

An internationally renowned artist, John Buckley, who has had exhibitions at museums of modern art in Paris, New York, Amsterdam, Berlin, London and Oxford, was also experimenting with ways to ask the same kinds of questions. John and I decided to join forces. The work of art that you see in New High Street today is the result. This piece of sculpture is a fundamental transformation of the house into a plinth for an object that challenges the very idea of what we mean by "home".

Through the creation of this sculpture we hoped to bring art out of the gallery, out from behind the high hedges of stately homes, out of the closed quadrangles of Oxford colleges. We wanted to bring art into the public street where people could live with it, feel it and respond to the power of that art. We wanted art to become part of everyday life, to make people look afresh at their environment and to enhance it.

Another aim was to make art accessible. We didn't want to present ideas and ask questions in a way that was cold, clinical and bypassable. John Buckley clearly put warmth and humour in his art to capture that moment where people don't know whether to gasp in surprise or laugh in delight. He combined serious views with humour, curiosity and the values of surrealism.

Did the sculptor succeed? Gloriously . . . and from so many angles. If you look at the sculpture from down the street near number 13 New High Street, you will see the underbelly of the Shark . . . the softer, whiter part . . . and a beautiful curve in the tail. As you come closer you notice the stomach muscles are ribbed at the shock of being ripped out of one element and plunged into another. The image has a sympathetic edge to it. One could feel respect for a beautiful, powerful animal and sorrow at its absurd predicament of being caught in the jaws of this house. The sculpture looks tame and almost tender from this angle and it's possible to imagine putting a small replica of the animal in the bathtub for your four-year-old child to play with.

When you walk up the street towards the house and move onto the intersection with the London Road, the whole aspect of the Shark changes. The dorsal fin emerges. The shape becomes much more angular and rigid. The curve in the tail disappears as the eye catches a different view. That lovely, sensuous arch of the body now seems to be a straight line with the precision of a carving knife. The pale gray, cream and pink of the soft underbelly give way to the deep dark colours of strange muscle and movement: rich purples, greens and blacks. The artist used over twenty coats of paint on the Shark to get the final blend of pigment and power. Now the Shark takes on a strange, steel-cold aspect and it's possible to imagine a large replica of the shape dropping from some aeroplane onto a city in Japan at the end of World War Two.

But the Shark isn't limited by any angle or any view. Like other great works of public sculpture the Shark is not just one thing, it's a richness of ideas. Nor is the Shark limited by time. Although it was created and erected in 1986 in response to certain events and ideas at that time, the sculpture has a source of energy that makes it as relevant now as the day it first went up, because the structure speaks of fundamental feelings and fears and ambivalence. The artist has torn the veil off conventional representations to make a strange beauty. Through the qualities and responses of this image, the artist confronts viewers with mirrors of their being in the world. Great art has the power to re-invent its own power and meaning for a new time and a new people.

Viewers constantly confirm this. They still pay their respects to the Shark. They still visit this sculpture in spite of some stiff competition from the jewels of rooftop architecture that crown one of the most splendid High Streets in Europe. Viewers create their own mythology for the Shark. Now in 1991 they re-invent the meaning of the sculpture as it relates to their hopes and fears and sense of wonder in Tokyo, Sydney, Johannesburg, Bogota and Birmingham.

Part of the power of the Shark is that it doesn't answer questions but rather presents us with new ways of seeing things. People respond to this challenge with a wealth of reactions that often start with a smile.

That smile is important because another aim of this sculpture was to give the people of Oxford and New High Street in particular, a gift, a surprise: and their acceptance of that gift is essential. The acceptance of any offering is as important as the giving. It was never my intention to inflict this sculpture on people. You can't simply put up a sculpture, cross your arms,

dig in your heels and ignore the reactions of people in the street who live with it. That would be something harmful and rightly controlled by planning laws. If people had rejected the Shark I would have taken it down by now. I wouldn't want to live in a street of resentment and anger caused by the sculpture. The approval of people was and is a key factor in the life of the Shark; and I made every effort to meet people, discuss the Shark and give them an opportunity to voice their opinions.

Within days of the Shark appearing in my roof, I wrote to all residents of the street and invited them to a tea party to discuss the sculpture and to hear their views. I was able to gauge public reaction by the many letters I received and by petitions to keep the Shark. I also conducted various surveys of opinion in New High Street. The result of these consultations and communications about the Shark undeniably indicates overwhelming support for the Shark to stay.

Within days of its arrival, the Shark was inspected thoroughly by a team of building control officers from the Oxford City Council who met with my structural engineer. The calculations of wind force and stress provided conclusive evidence that the Shark was a safe structure and the Oxford City Building Control Officer, Mr Frank Black, issued a certificate stating that the Shark met all the structural requirements and tests of the law.

Indeed the sculpture has stood the test of time and withstood the onslaught of the hurricane in 1987. In aerodynamic terms this Shark is impeccable.

Opponents claimed the Shark would be a target for vandals and young *hooligans would attack it, especially since it was sited so close to the Oxford United football ground which is less than two hundred yards away. They said people would not respect the Shark and would deface it with paint and graffiti.*

There is evidence to show that putting art in public places does not encourage vandalism but in fact deters it. Art makes an area "special" and in a way art "tames" a place and indicates that this area is to be treated with respect. There are many examples of where art in public places has helped to reclaim the area for the public from the vandals.

With reference to the Shark, this sculpture has certainly made its surrounding area of New High Street special and no one has even attempted to treat it with disrespect. Perhaps this is due in no small part to the fact that most people in the Street no longer talk about this sculpture as "the" Shark. They now refer to it as "our" Shark. They have personalised its value and made it a part of their environment.'

Up to this point I've described events from my point of view, but I still need to address the Council's point of view, which has never quite made sense to me.

'Finally Oxford City Council complains that the sculpture has a harmful effect on the appearance of the building and on the street scene in new High Street. But what exactly does the council mean by this? What is the basis of their complaint?

Do they object to the colour? I've not heard that anyone was offended by the subtle hues and shadings. The careful brush strokes of cream and silk and pink and echoes of blue merge with a myriad of gray, green and black. Not one person has objected to the way the colours complement each other and reflect the sea of grey roof slates from which the Shark's tail emerges. The skill in the use of colour is particularly evident during adverse weather conditions. On a cloudy day the sculpture recedes slightly into the background yet the colours are still distinct. The choice and use of colour is quiet, understated, rich and complex. Clearly this could not possibly be the basis of the complaint.

What about the texture? Any complaints about that? The sculpture is a complicated network of sleek, smooth tail scales, almost silken fin texture, sandpapered dorsal, and ribbed underbelly. Once again not a single voice has been raised against the skill and subtlety of the texture. This could hardly be grounds for a complaint.

◤ *Are the materials used in the sculpture the basis of the objection?* The sculpture is not made of rough concrete or new bricks that jar with the house or mar the site. The Shark consists of seamless fibreglass that does not call attention to itself and yet when painted by the artist has a combination of softness and strength, hardness and clarity of line that makes the choice of material one that is sympathetic with the roof slates and the house. Clearly this also is not the source of the irritation.

◤ *Craftsmanship and design?* Would the Council argue that the design is inferior? The sculpture was created by a professional artist who has been working in clay, bronze and fibreglass for over a quarter of a century. His experience, skill and talent are stamped on every inch of this work of art. The construction and use of materials could hardly have been of a higher standard. Obviously this is not the basis of the objection.

◤ *Scale? Is this the problem?* The relationship of the house and the roof to the width, height and incline of the sculpture is at the very heart of why so many people find delight and meaning in the Shark. The scale, the relationship of the Shark to the space and built environment around it is central to the concerns of the artist. The sculpture has been carefully created to ring with a resonance to all the other aspects of the house. The width and height relate to the total roof space of the part of the terrace where the Shark resides, to the windows, the door, the green gate and the backdrop of the nearby trees. Even the wooden electric cable mast on the footpath outside the house is important to the size and scale of the sculpture.

You may have noticed that the part of this terrace where the Shark is located has no chimneys. The new, modern brick structure next door to the Shark house, Number 2A, the Shark House itself and the four flats at Number 4 New High Street do not any longer have vertical lines on the roof in the form of chimneys, even though chimneys have come to be seen as an important part of the scale of a house. The vertical lines of these pipes and cowls break up the horizontal mass of the houses. That part of the terrace which is home to the Shark does not have these important structures which often help to create an harmonious appearance of any terrace. The sculpture adds those vertical lines which enhance the house and exert a pleasing and balancing effect in relation to the terrace.

Although the City Council claims the sculpture is a large and prominent feature in the street, they do not claim that it is out of scale with the other features of the area. The scale therefore is clearly not the basis of their objection.

Is it the subject matter of the sculpture to which opponents object? Do some Oxford City Councillors object to this sculpture because it is a Shark and they think that is absurd? If the artist used the same colouring, texture, materials, craftsmanship and scale on a structure of a different subject matter, like for instance a church steeple, would that be a development acceptable to the City Council for New High Street?

If that is the case, if the City Council is objecting to the subject matter, then I suggest the Council is trying to impose its own sense of aesthetic judgement and propriety and is stepping outside the bounds of proper planning criteria and has no legitimate grounds for objection.'

I believe I have dealt with every question, angle or issue about the Shark. But no, there is one more question to which the barrister for Oxford City Council requires an answer. He wants to know – Do I sleep in the house? And I tell him – 'not always'. Then he cross-examines me at length trying to find out where and with whom I sleep. 'Are you married? If you are not married do you have a partner? Do you have a family?'

This doesn't go down well with one member of the public at the Inquiry. Margaret Crallen writes: 'I could have killed the barrister who interrogated you on Tuesday and didn't even have the courtesy to look at you while he was speaking. His attempt to disconcert you by referring to your private life was *unforgiveable'*.

I choose not to be offended because I believe this, like so many other actions of Oxford City Council in this saga, is strange, surreal and completely beside the point; and I'm still left with that *Butch Cassidy and The Sundance Kid* question – 'Who *are* those guys?'

'Parrhots and owwls!'

A Public Inquiry is a rigid and formal event where adversaries sit on opposing sides in the Oxford Town Hall, facing each other behind barristers in wigs and clerks with bushels of books, and beneath a judge-like person elevated a few feet higher than the rest of us. It is a stage-managed event, but every once in a while strange things can happen.

Someone I had not met before enters the hall and asks to address the Inquiry. John Blackwood introduces himself as a local resident and writer of several books including one on the gargoyles and grotesques of Oxford. There is something of the gargoyle about this man. He brings the unexpected into play – a slight person with a big voice, a serious face with deep laugh-lines, a shy person who has a sting in his tale.

'These carvings, some of which have served
Oxford for hundreds of years, are no less surprising and
shocking in their appearance and context than the Headington Shark.'

Mr Blackwood explains that his book on the Oxford grotesque tradition appeared just a few months before the Headington Shark and is now known in almost as many countries of the world – indicating the important role these carvings play in Oxford and what an extraordinary appeal they have, both to residents and to visitors.

'My submission is this – the Headington Shark is not an erratic, one-off work, intriguing and even popular in the short term but in the long term somewhat trivial. I suggest that it occupies a firm place in a very long tradition of architectural decoration here in Oxford, that is to say in the tradition of the grotesque. Whether Mr Heine intended to be so traditional, I do not know; from his remarks yesterday about breaking away from the closed world of the Oxford quadrangle, I would suppose not.

Nevertheless, this is what he and Mr Buckley have achieved. The more I think about it, the clearer it becomes that here we have an object which in its appearance and its relationship to the surroundings fulfils very much the same purposes as the several thousand carvings which cluster on the churches and colleges of this ancient city.'

He holds up a picture of one of Oxford's oldest grotesques which comes from Merton Chapel, at the base of one of the columns, and dates from around 1300:

'This Green Man has a tree growing from its nostrils and appears as a kind of demi-god of Nature, but as Nature in its horrific, sacrificial aspect. Some scholars argue that the projecting tongue indicates the head is being hung, suspended in a noose. The Green Man evokes just the same kind of atavistic, natural terrors as does that wild and ruthless creature, the predatory Shark.'

Then he moves on six and a half centuries and looks at another kind of fish:

'This recently carved figure is to be found on the outside of New College Chapel. But what is such a goggle-eyed, sharp-toothed, crested monster doing on a building of worship? How alien, indeed, how discordant? And if you find the fish shocking, then try out a monkey. This vulgar beast squats directly above the main entrance to that venerable seat of learning, Magdalen College and, quite clearly, he is urinating into the drain head.

These carvings, some of which have served Oxford for hundreds of years, are no less surprising and shocking in their appearance and context than the Headington Shark. But some obvious objections could be made to that comparison and I wish to answer them straightaway.

First, one might argue that the carvings are old and the Shark is new. A great number of Oxford's grotesques were put up during the restorations of the last thirty years and a good two dozen are of more recent date than the Shark.

However, you may say they are not nearly as prominent. It is true that the majority impress by their variety and number rather than their size; but there are eight giant grotesques protruding along one side of Merton chapel and each is several feet long and weighs over a ton. Also the Emperors' heads in a high ring around the Sheldonian Theatre are a highly prominent and celebrated example of staring, glaring old men with a bewildering array of beards.

Just look at the more than twenty statues in Magdalen's Cloister Quad, look at the monstrosity of each one eight or nine feet high on its pedestal. Yet dons and students live daily looking out at them; for an Oxford quadrangle is indeed, par excellence, a quiet residential area.

But you may say, these carvings fit in with their surroundings; we know their style, we are used to them. My point is that you should not be used to them. Must we have a presumption in favour of dullness? If you look carefully and intelligently at what is actually there, you cannot fail to be shocked and amazed. And if you are also shocked and amazed (as well as delighted) by the Headington Shark, then Mr Buckley has succeeded in reviving and revivifying an old tradition.

So why are these carvings there? What is really behind them? This is a complex question, especially since their medieval originators left us no explanations of what they were doing. But yesterday when Mr Heine so movingly recounted how he was impelled to erect the Shark as a response to the bombing of homes in Tripoli and to the Chernobyl explosion, I heard a familiar chord being struck. How can we express the true evil, the horror in life, the underside, the penumbra of chaos which always surrounds, except indirectly, using the weapons of humour and the distortion of physical appearance?

I am simply referring to the physical appearance of certain Oxford buildings, and their attendant decorations which can be judged and understood only in and on their buildings. Thus just as the potentially one-sided piety and learning of Oxford's Gothic colleges is balanced and made more sane by the eccentricity and humour of its carvings, so the potentially self-complacent security of a Headington terrace house is challenged by a Shark descending through its roof – and not only challenged but rendered more poignant, more to be valued in a truly uncertain world.

It is not my task to analyse the debates which have gone on in the City Council about the Shark; that has been done by others. However, I have formed the distinct impression that it is not the whole Council which opposes Mr Heine but a part of it. And that part has a strong leader, namely the Chairman of Oxford City Planning Committee, Mr John Power. Now in this context Mr Power reminds me very much of St Bernard of Clairvaux, founder of the Cistercian Order, councillor of princes and inspirer of, I think, the First Crusade.

However, St Bernard had a blind spot when it came to grotesques. In 1125, as the new architectural movement was just getting into its stride, he wrote a furious letter to a colleague:

"Of what use to the brothers reading piously in the cloisters are these ridiculous monstrosities, these prodigies of deformed beauty, these beautiful deformities? There on one body grow several heads, and several bodies have one head. Here a quadruped wears the head of a serpent, and the head of a quadruped appears on the body of a fish. Almighty God! If we are not ashamed of these unclean things, we should at least regret what we have spent on them."

Well, are we not glad, looking back, that St Bernard did not succeed in strangling Gothic carving at birth?

I am also reminded, much closer to home, of Dr Plumptre, who was instrumental in the building of the University Museum as a neo-Gothic temple of knowledge in the 1850s. Famous carvers, the brothers O'Shea from Dublin, were brought in to decorate the building. Their exquisite renderings of plant species may be seen on the interior columns. Around the outsides of the windows they were set to carve the world's fauna. Their free-ranging, gargoyle-like style did not appeal to everyone. Dr Acland, Professor of Medicine, and the other chief pillar behind the project, tells this story:

"O'Shea rushed into my home one afternoon and, in a state of wild excitement, told this tale: Dr Plumptre found me on my scaffold just now. 'What are you doing?', says he. 'Monkeys,' says I. 'Come down directly,' says he, 'you shall not destroy the property of the University.'

Despite this O'Shea was back at the window the following day carving cats, and he succeeded in frightening Dr Plumptre away with his protests. It could not last. Soon afterwards, all the carvers were dismissed and as a result two-thirds of the windows have remained forever blank.

However, O'Shea was determined to have one last throw and Dr Acland found him striking furiously at some pillars inside the porch. 'What are you doing?' he asked. Striking on, O'Shea explained that he was caricaturing the dignitaries who had dismissed him.

'Parrhots and Owwls!' he cried. 'Parrhots and Owwls! Members of Convocation!'"

And indeed, O'Shea's birds may still be seen roughed out in the porch, as a warning against intolerant and arbitrary planning decisions.

I feel confident that in our present case those in positions of influence and authority will not behave like parrots or owls. They will not mechanically repeat and unthinkingly impose restrictive planning formulae nor will they, like owls, blink stupefied before the light of vision, wit and imagination.'

The big voice trails off. This slight man nods to the judge-like figure and sits down. There is complete, stunned silence.

By hook or by crook

Brian Hook and Janet Todd both ask to address the Public Inquiry and both have powerful stories about why the Shark should go; but the stories of this odd couple are flawed.

Brian Hook is an architect 'working from an office directly opposite the Shark'. Mr Hook lays out his stall very carefully by describing the Shark: 'It is extremely clever. The Shark defies gravity. It also defies good taste, enforcement orders and the elected representatives and has done so for five years. It is a brilliant piece of effrontery. It is pure showmanship. The Shark is totally out of scale with that particular street.'

When the Shark arrived five years ago, Mr Hook wrote to Oxford City Council 'to express my extreme concern about the extraordinary structure which has been placed on the roof of the property opposite my office in New High Street.' He also pointed out that 'clients of mine have been refused planning permission for very inoffensive small flat lettering on first-floor offices in Oxford. The planning authority takes the view that first-floor lettering, even if it is small "will be prominent, intrusive and detrimental to the visual amenity of the area". Sharks are a different kettle of fish but even more intrusive!'

Mr Hook says he has to 'put up' with the Shark every day and he has never been approached or spoken to by me. The barrister for Oxford City Council, David Rundell, turns to me and demands to know why I haven't spoken to my nearest neighbour, the person directly opposite who has to look at the Shark every day.

I'm delighted he has asked that question and I'm pleased to make the acquaintance of Mr Hook, 'my most immediate neighbour'. Several times over the last five years I've knocked on the office door opposite my house and every time the person who opened the door was a staff member from a charity known as NORCAP which helps abandoned babies eventually find their birth parents. I'm pleased to report that they are all strong supporters of the Shark.

Mr Hook rents out the property. I've never met him over the past five years because he doesn't work in an office opposite my house, he works in a village called Kingston Bagpuize about ten miles away from the Shark, so he doesn't have to 'put up' with the Shark each day. His client who was refused planning permission for very small, inoffensive lettering was in fact Mr Hook himself.

I reach out my hand and tell him it's very good to meet, even though it is in a Public Inquiry where he is making some questionable comments about my Shark.

Mrs Janet Todd makes a very good fist of her argument. She admits she does not live in New High Street, but she goes to Church there every Sunday. Since she is the leader of the Conservatives on Oxford City Council, her political as well as her religious instincts point to a deep disturbance caused by the Shark. Mrs Todd is over 80 years of age, an advocate for the elderly and friend to residents at nearby Alison Clay House, the sheltered accommodation block.

> 'These poor old people are desperately unhappy with the Shark as a neighbour. This is the end of the generation that served in the War. We owe them at least peace and contentment in their old age. But the Shark has shattered this. In some cases they can't get on with their lives because this big, grey blot is hanging over them, almost literally.
>
> The Shark is a personal intrusion into their space. They feel invaded. Each one of these residents is upset that anyone would do this to them. It has caused deep strain and stress in people who are old, frail or infirm. They have had to live in the shadow of a threat, which is exactly how many of them see the Shark. This is not fair or reasonable. In fact it's downright cruel to keep that thing defacing what once was a very good roof. As the years go by they are getting more and more wound up. Most of them hate the Shark. It is absolutely awful. If Mr Heine knew the distress that Shark is causing his neighbours at Alison Clay House, he would take it down this instant. Shame on him.'

It is a performance that moves me and everyone else at the Inquiry. If I am doing this kind of damage, it's time to take the Shark down. This is a hard way to end the first day of the Public Inquiry, and I think it is a turning point.

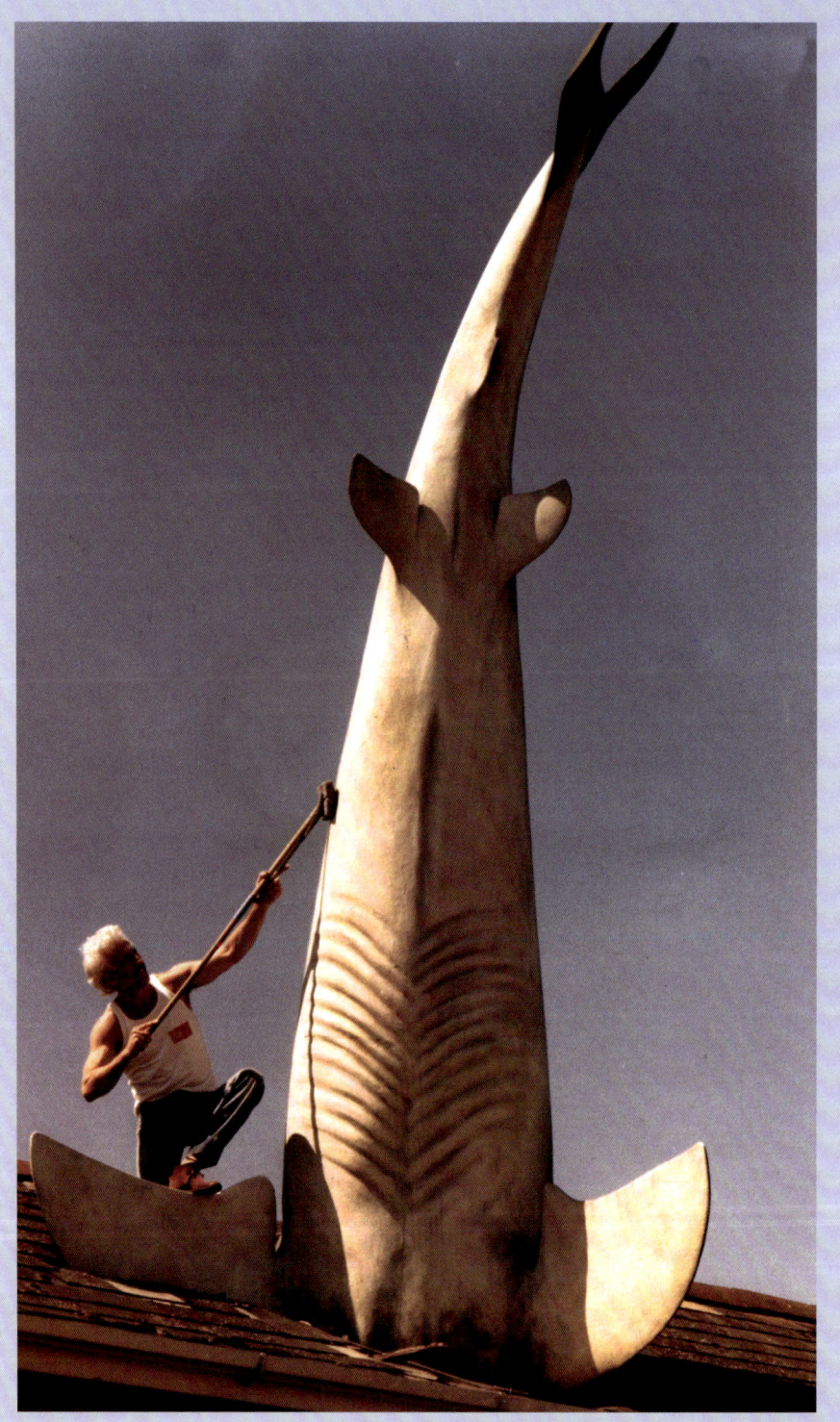

The second day starts with a jolt. We can hear it coming. Entry to the venue of the Inquiry is not easy. People with disabilities may have difficulties. A small woman, with a chalk-yellow face and bending way too far forward, enters the room pushing her Zimmer frame.

15

She doesn't want to attract attention and with slow deliberation she mounts the steps to the visitors' area and sits in her Zimmer on the edge of a row of seats. When she is composed and ready, she catches the eye of the clerk and says she would like to speak. She starts slowly with a low voice, barely audible. 'I apologise for my appearance and I'm a bit out of breath, but I wasn't expecting to be here today. I've come from my sick bed.'

She grasps the handles of her Zimmer frame and with the nervous energy of a child giving a recital she inches forward until she is in danger of tumbling down the stairs.

'My name is Rosy Grace. I'm a resident at Alison Clay House. While I was lying in bed this morning I listened to the local news on BBC Radio Oxford. They said that the residents of Alison Clay House are all strongly opposed to the Shark. Well, I'm here to tell you first of all that I think the Shark is great . . . and so do others, but they don't want to cause trouble for themselves so they keep quiet.

There has been a petition against the Shark and many residents have signed, but in some cases, they don't know what they've signed. The organisers, of course, put pressure on people and I know personally that several people did not want to put their signatures on the petition, but they signed under duress. I also know that if some residents didn't have the Shark to complain about, they would find something else.

This story of Alison Clay House against the Shark is wrong, and it has been wrong for a long time. Three years ago a neighbour in the street wanted to gain access to Alison Clay House and circulate a petition in favour of the Shark, but she was refused entry.

One of the earlier petitions contained the name of a friend of mine, Dot Hall. The organiser decided to present the petition at a City Council meeting and collected signatures on two days when Dot Hall was away from Alison Clay House, so she couldn't have signed. I have the petition here and the name of D. Hall you see is a forgery. I also have her true signature on another sheet so you can compare for yourself.

Opponents to the Shark will do almost anything to get rid of it, and this latest attack I heard on the radio this morning is wrong. I want to put that right.'

After delivering this warning, she sank back down in her Zimmer and the Inquiry continued. But the sculptor John Buckley is convinced that this is the moment when the debate was over. I'm not so sure.

'Quite contrary'

After two turbulent days of a Public Inquiry, the Shark enjoys a period of calm weather – like the eye of a hurricane, still waters made even more eerie by the thunder and lightning that has just passed.

We have no choice but to sit tight and await the decision on the future of the Shark by Secretary of State for the Environment Michael Heseltine. But that doesn't stop the speculation.

The *Oxford Times* cuts through the tension and publishes this article entitled 'Quite Contrary' with the by-line – '*Peter McIntyre has an exclusive story about a well-known fish*'.

> '*An inspector appointed by the Secretary of State for the Environment recently heard the appeal against the removal of the Oxford Shark. Here, exclusively, we reveal a leaked copy of his report.*
>
> *Dear Mr Heseltine,*
>
> *I recently spent a couple of pleasant days in Oxford hearing evidence for and against the removal of a large fishlike object protruding upwards from the roof of a house in New High Street, Headington.*
>
> *I quickly decided that this case boiled down to two questions:*
>
> *1. Does the Shark have a head inside the roof?*
>
> *2. Does the roof leak?*
>
> *I would have recommended pulling the Shark down, until I heard the council. Their view is that if Mr Heine is allowed to keep it, then everyone will want one.*
>
> *If the council is right this would have solved your Poll Tax problem. You could simply have introduced a roof tax, based on the size of your fish and have done with it. However, the Shark has been in situ for many years and even people with Sky TV don't seem to want one.*
>
> *My conclusions are as follows: The Shark was designed by sculptor John Buckley and installed by Mr Heine, who are responsible for a pair of*

arms and a head at the Penultimate Picture Palace and some kicking legs at the Not The Moulin Rouge Cinema. These two men are clearly obsessed with the end bits of bodies, expressing their unconscious wish for sudden endings.

Mr Heine's campaign to save the Shark is, sub-consciously, a poignant plea to see it pulled down. The council on the other hand has everything to lose by removing the Shark. Without it people might spend more time asking them about homelessness, riots etc. The council's suppressed desire is therefore that the Shark should stay. Moreover, if planning permission is granted it is likely that Mr Heine and Mr Buckley will take it down, since the artistic merit of a fish that is allowed is negligible.

I conclude, therefore, that the Shark be given a Preservation Order (satisfying the council) but that planning permission be refused and that the council issue periodic threats to remove it (satisfying Mr Heine).

This would have settled the matter if my attention had not been drawn to the rather drab brick premises in which the Shark resides, a house, utterly devoid of contemporary artistic merit. Although the Shark must stay, the house must go.

Finally, Mr Heseltine, I ask you to consider the artistic message of the Shark, which is that in this world no event is too strange to rule out. It is my closing conclusion that you entirely disregard my report and make a decision that will be widely seen as arbitrary, unfair and devoid of reason. I leave this task in your hands with some confidence.'

The Shark, by now quite long in the tooth, slowly makes her way through layers of government bureaucracy leaving a trail of disturbance and disagreement in her wake. The Inspector from the Planning Inquiry takes the favourable view of keeping the Shark, but officials in the Ministry of Planning take exception. Several months later the Shark arrives on the desk of the Senior Planning Minister Sir George Young with a big red stamp on it recommending 'Rejection'.

The bureaucrats accept the copy-cat argument in its extreme form. 'The appeal should be disallowed . . . otherwise the country's skyline would be dominated by millions of wavering dorsal fins and tails as the new ruling was exploited. The very integrity of the planning system would be challenged.'

HOUSE OF FRASER HOLDINGS plc

Media Department: Chairman's Office, Harrods Limited
Knightsbridge, London SW1X 7XL
Telephone : 071-584 3930   Fax: 071-581 1593

Mr. Bill Heine,
2 New High Street,
Headington,
OXFORD.   28 May 1992

Dear Mr. Heine,

Mr. Al Fayed, the Chairman of Harrods has asked me to write on
his behalf and congratulate you -- one shark owner to another --
upon your recent historic and thoroughly deserved victory over
the planners.

Mr. Al Fayed hopes that you will take the opportunity when in
London to visit the Food Halls at Harrods in order to see the
real thing as against the fibreglass replica. I enclose a
photograph of "Tiny" the shark -- named after some businessman
or other who has been known to display the characteristics of a
shark in the past but has now lost some of his teeth in old age.
Mr. Al Fayed wishes you to know that if you name your creation
"Tiny 2" he would be gratified and regard it as a compliment.

I know Mr. Al Fayed has followed your saga with interest and
although the poet may never have been moved by the "dreaming fish
tails of Oxford" he feels that your humour has added interest to
the skyline and given many people amusement.

Kind regards,

Yours sincerely,

Michael Cole
Director of Public Affairs

Registered Office: 1 Howic
Registered in Eng

On the morning of 21 May, 1992 at 9.30 I am on air at BBC Radio Oxford during a three-hour programme till noon. I see through the studio windows that some kind of bomb has exploded under my producer, Stewart Woodcock, and his staff. They are all leaping around answering telephones, shouting instructions, typing notes and talking on the intercom. More staff from other programmes arrive to help. It's bedlam.

16

'YOUR SHARK'S OK'

I'm in the middle of a live debate about fox hunting when Stewart barks into my headphones – 'Your Shark's OK.' I don't get it at first. Then he shouts – 'You're on your own mate. I'm dealing with the *New York Times*, Reuters, the *Guardian*, *Der Spiegel* and the *Sydney Morning Herald*.'

At the top of the hour I cross over to the news desk and their lead story confirms the cause of the chaos. The new Secretary of State for the Environment, Michael Howard, has announced the Shark is free to float forever among the spires of Oxford. It has been granted planning permission.

Mistakes happen; I need to see this in writing. Is it really true? My solicitor sends me the original documents from the Planning Inspector, Peter MacDonald, who doesn't duck the issues:

> *'Into this archetypal suburban setting crashes (almost literally) the Shark. The contrast between the object and its setting is quite deliberate. In this sense, the work is specific to its setting, and it would 'read' quite differently in the context of, say, the foyer to an arts centre in Gloucester*

A city trader out shark hunting in Mauritius got in touch with Harrods owner Mohamed al-Fayed and asked him if he'd like a Mako shark for his store. Mohamed said yes and the taxidermed specimen was sent over to Harrods where it was hung over the fish counter. It was given the name 'Tiny' on its fin – after 'Tiny' Rowlands, a rival businessman with whom Mr al-Fayed had had several business dealings including the convoluted purchase of Harrods. In 1992 peace broke out between the two men and the shark was ceremoniously lowered, much to the amusement of passers-by and press. It was intended to be delivered to 'Tiny's' home to hang over his swimming pool, but Mr al-Fayed pursuaded him to auction it off for charity, where it was bought by a marine attraction park owner for £2.500 – the proceeds going to Great Ormond St Hospital Children's Charity.

Courtesy of the Oxford Mail/Oxford Times (Newsquest Oxfordshire)

"A FIBRE GLASS SHARK THAT HAS ADORNED A ROOF FOR SIX YEARS CAN REMAIN AS A SYMBOL OF REBELLION AGAINST DRAB UNIFORMITY..." *(News Item)*

Local and national Press tap into the shark's victory. The Garland cartoon (above) featured in the *Daily Telegraph* 23rd May, 1992. Jim Needle's cartoons (top) were an *Oxford Star* staple at the time.

Green. It is (as the Council say) incongruous, and that incongruity is quite consciously sought by the artist. It is, indeed, out of harmony with its surrounds. It is that lack of harmony, that sense of being 'out of place', to which the Council objects, and which it equates with demonstrable harm to visual amenity. It is the very same feature which appeals to many of the Shark's supporters, and which has made it an urban landmark . . . An "incongruous" object can become accepted as a landmark in some cases, becoming well-known, even well-loved, in the process. Something of this sort seems to have happened, for many people, to the Shark.

There is a real sense in which permitting the Shark to remain is the "risky" option, the safe and easy thing to do being to remove it. However, I cannot believe that the purpose of planning control is to enforce a boring and mediocre uniformity on the built environment. Any system of control must make some small space for the dynamic, the unexpected and the downright quirky, or we shall all be the poorer for it. I believe that this is one case where a little vision and imagination is appropriate, and I recommend that the Headington Shark be allowed to remain.'

The Junior Planning Minister, Tony Baldry, MP for Banbury, announces the decision in an up-beat manner – 'The planning system is not intended to introduce a sense of dull uniformity.'

The Senior Planning Minister, Sir George Young, says that when his 'Yes, Minister' officials said 'no' to the Shark: 'I demurred. While I don't want to be surrounded by plastic fish at roof top level, I did want to live in a country where some eccentric can put half a Shark in his attic without being steamrollered by an insensitive bureaucracy.'

The reaction to this decision is instantaneous. Poet Rip Bulkeley is inspired to pen   Lines on the Occasion . . . etc.

My heart leaps up when I behold
A sea-shark in the sky.
So was it when one first appeared,
So is it now the thing's been cleared,
So let it be while years unfold
And fish fly by.

Bernard Levin, probably the greatest journalist of his day, exorates Oxford City Council and praises the Shark in *The Times*, while cartoonists have a field day.

Bernard Levin

A fibreglass shark plunging into an Oxford rooftop is a lark that baffles officialdom

I start unkindly, I fear, by saying that Mr John Power, who is chairman of the planning committee of Oxford city council, might do well to go and boil his head in a light stock with a *bouquet garni* and perhaps a teaspoonful of sherry.

This discourtesy is provoked by Mr Power sounding off in no uncertain manner: "... a victory for anarchy ... a slap in the face for the decent and respectable people ... seeking legal advice ..." And what has brought him, in his municipal character, to such a state? Has someone opened a brothel next door to Balliol? Has the Sheldonian been taken over by meths-drinking dossers? Or has a band of undergraduate scofflaws had the impudence to debag Mr Power himself and paint his bottom purple?

No such luck. What has brought Mr Power to the very edge of bursting is the decision of the public enquiry into the Hunting of the Shark. Over the six years of battle, you must have seen photographs of the famous fish which adorns the roof of the Oxford house of a Mr Bill Heine (to whom goes the Diamond Star and Sash of the Order of They Shall Be Mocked and With Good Reason); made of fibreglass, it is sited to look as though the shark dived headfirst at the roof-tiles and crashed through up to its gills. It makes a delightful, innocent, fresh and amusing sculpture, and people come from far and wide to see it, to admire it, to photograph it, and to smile at it.

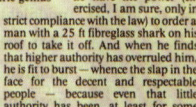

A fishy tale: monument to an eccentric genius

But there is nothing about smiling in the analects of the planning committee of the Oxford city council, and that august body ruled that it must come down, giving as the reason that it had been put up without planning permission, or more likely just because it *was* delightful, innocent, fresh and amusing — all qualities abhorred by such committees. Mr Heine (if he is descended from Heinrich Heine, it is another reason for me to shake his hand) fought heroically through the years as the battle swayed this way and that, with the authorities getting more and more indignant at the impudence of a mere person defying the might of a planning committee.

It had to go to a public enquiry, and eventually did, whence the sound of corks popping at 2 New High Street, Headington. For not only did the planning inspector of the Department of the Environment, Mr Peter Macdonald, rule that the shark can stay where it is, but the decision was couched in language so human, so intelligent and so wise that it ought to be painted in enormous letters on the pavements (both sides) of Whitehall. Here are some of his conclusions: "I cannot believe that the purpose of planning control is to enforce a boring and mediocre uniformity ... Any system of control must make some space for the dynamic, the unexpected and the downright quirky, or we shall all be the poorer for it. I believe that this is one case where a little vision and imagination is appropriate." Whereupon, Mr Power made it clear that he would "try to challenge the decision", a threat that brought from Lord Palumbo, chairman of the Arts Council, this mild but appallingly true comment: "Most politicians do not know how to lose graciously."

When I am Ruler of the Universe, one of my earliest decrees will lay down that anyone who uses the words "What if everybody did it?" will be fed to Sirius, the dog star. It is the last resort of the fun-killers, the oriflamme of the pursed lips brigade, the buttress of those whose motto is "Go and see what Johnny is doing and tell him to stop it". Anyone but a prize nana would have seen that Mr Heine's splendid lark (I pause here to commend the sculptor, Mr John Buckley) was an exact definition of delight, particularly Shakespeare's kind "that give delight and hurt not".

But it hurt the planning committee no end, whence the six years of battle and the preposterous comments ("... a slap in the face of the decent and respectable people ...") of its chairman when the battle was finally lost and won.

It is not difficult to see how people get things so devastatingly out of scale; indeed it is one of the most thoroughly studied of human frailties. I poked fun at the Oxford council planning committee and in particular its chairman, but that was largely because I had a measure of that body — useful but nothing more. Now suppose you have worked hard and honestly at your job (useful but nothing more), and you dream, or once did dream, of making a mighty stir, of climbing to the heights, of being Someone. What is the inevitable knowledge that goes with what has happened to those dreams, and what can be done about it? The knowledge, of course, is that the dreams have not come true; what can be done about it is to exercise that tiny corner of the world in which you *do* hold sway.

Man, proud man, dressed in a little brief authority ... Shakespeare knew humankind, and knew that the briefer the authority the greater the vigour with which it is employed. The chairman of the Oxford council planning committee does not have the power to have anybody's head cut off, nor to have anybody exiled to Outer Mongolia, nor even to compel anybody to do penance in a white sheet for seven days and seven nights. But he and his council *do* have the power (exercised, I am sure, only in strict compliance with the law) to order a man with a 25 ft fibreglass shark on his roof to take it off. And when he finds that higher authority has overruled him, he is fit to burst — whence the slap in the face for the decent and respectable people — because even that little authority has been, at least for some time, taken from him.

Shun power, shun it fiercely, if you want to sleep soundly in your bed. If it is real power, the power to compel others to do your bidding, your dreams will be haunted ones. If it is the mock power of the chairmanship of a municipal committee in Oxford, you will wake to disappointment. I am not going to quote Acton, but here is Hazlitt, who in this context is even more apposite:

> The love of liberty is the love of others; the love of power is the love of ourselves.

You do not have to be a bad man to want power. Our chairman is plainly an honest and scrupulous man, certainly to be numbered among the decent and respectable people who have figured so largely in this story. But he has forgotten the old and tried proverb: "A man with a stuffed shark on his roof is eccentric, and quite possibly in breach of the planning rules; a man who tries to take the shark off will run no danger of being bitten, but will almost certainly make a fool of himself."

Victory ... Bill Heine in the shadow of the shark

Rooftop Jaws wins battle for survival

THE rooftop shark of Headington won its battle for survival today.

Environment Secretary Michael Howard ruled that the 25ft-high sculpture can stay on the tiles in New High Street where it has delighted and infuriated people in almost equal measure for the past six years.

The decision brought jubilation for the shark's owner, Radio Oxford presenter Bill Heine, who commissioned the work from

He said: "It is wonderful news. If the shark ever dies now it will be because of old age, not because someone killed it.

"People will be able to enjoy it well into the next century."

But there was a furious reaction from the Oxford planning committee chairman John Power who has led the fight against the fish.

He told the Oxford Mail: "This is a victory for anarchy.

"It is a slap in the face for the decent and respectable people

John Power, Chairman of Oxford City Planning Committee, is apoplectic:

'The decision to allow the Shark to stay is a victory for anarchy and a defeat for the forces of law and order. I am asking the City solicitor to consider appealing against the decision on a point of law.

I think that since the Secretary of State [for the Environment] agrees in his report that the Shark is large, prominent and out of character with its surrounds, the appeal should not have been allowed. After all we are constantly refusing people permission to make alterations to their houses for those very reasons.'

One local resident has some advice for John Power, Alan Stopp writes to the editor of the *Oxford Courier*:

'City planning chief John Power should look at things which are more to the point i.e. the beggars on the streets of the city and the drunks who cause problems to visitors and locals. The Shark is a plus to the City. Mr Power talks about law-abiding citizens. He is so out of touch it is laughable. I have one message for him: If he can't stand the heat get out of the kitchen and get his priorities in the right order.'

The *Oxford Mail*, on the other hand, supports Mr Power with an editorial entitled 'A Bad Decision':

'Oxford city council should take whatever action it can to overturn the ludicrous ruling by Environment Secretary Michael Howard that the rooftop Shark in Headington, which nosedives through the roof of a house owned by BBC Radio Oxford presenter Bill Heine, can stay. Mr Howard's decision makes fools of Oxford's planners, whose chairman John Power is rightly incensed by it. He points out with some justification that the Shark sculpture was put up without planning permission, which was applied for later, and makes a mockery of planning procedures which are adhered to by most people and businesses. Mr Heine maintains the Shark is a work of art. It smacks more of a wind-up. It is certainly an oddity which has caused heated debate. But the fact is that Mr Howard's ruling has opened the doors to anyone who wants to flout the planning rules laid down by his own Government.

There is an alternative. Mr Heine has had his fun, at considerable cost to the taxpayers who met the bill for the legal processes in the long fight to preserve planning principles. He should now offer his so-called work of art to the City to be displayed on a more environmentally friendly site.'

Six months later, after Mr Power has asked his planning officers to go through the full report with a fine-tooth comb for faults, he is still attacking 'this cock-eyed decision'.

Since the deadline has long passed when the City Council can challenge the decision on legal grounds, Mr Power asks the Parliamentary Ombudsman to look at the case and launch an official investigation.

John Power is the Captain Ahab in the hunting of the Shark and it's not hard to get the measure of him; but *The Times* columnist, Bernard Levin, catches the flavour of the man and the moral of the tale and delivers a well constructed article on the awfulness of petty power, the smiling effect of the Shark (except with the planning committee) and how he would like to shake my hand . . .

'I start unkindly, I fear, by saying that Mr John Power, who is Oxford City Council Planning Committee Chairman might do well to go and boil his head in a light stock with a bouquet garni and perhaps a teaspoonful of sherry.

This discourtesy is provoked by Mr Power sounding off in no uncertain manner: ". . . a victory for anarchy. . . a slap in the face for the decent and respectable people . . . seeking legal advice. . ." And what has brought him, in his municipal character, to such a state? Has someone opened a brothel next door to Balliol? Has the Sheldonian been taken over by meths-drinking dossers? Or has a band of undergraduate scofflaws had the impudence to debag Mr Power himself and paint his bottom purple?

No such luck. What has brought Mr Power to the very edge of bursting is the decision of the public inquiry into the Hunting of the Shark. Over the six years of battle, you must have seen photographs of the famous fish which adorns the roof of the Oxford house of a Mr Bill Heine (to whom goes the Diamond Star and Sash of the Order of They Shall Be Mocked and With Good Reason); made of fibreglass, it is sited to look as though the Shark dived headfirst at the roof-tiles and crashed through up to its gills. It makes a delightful, innocent, fresh and amusing sculpture, and people come from far and wide to see it, to admire it, to photograph it, and to smile at it.

But there is nothing about smiling in the analects of Oxford City Council Planning Committee, and that august body ruled that it must come down, giving as the reason that it had been put up without planning permission, or more likely just because it was delightful, innocent, fresh and amusing – all qualities abhorred by such committees. Mr Heine (If he is descended from Heinrich Heine, it is another reason for me to shake his hand) fought heroically through the years as the battle swayed this way and that, with the authorities getting more and more indignant at the impudence of a mere person defying the might of a planning committee.

It had to go to a public inquiry, and eventually did, whence the sound of corks popping at 2 New High Street, Headington. For not only did the Planning Inspector, Mr Peter MacDonald, rule that the Shark can stay where it is, but the decision was couched in language so human, so intelligent and so wise that it ought to be painted in enormous letters on the pavements (both sides) of Whitehall. Here are some of his conclusions: "I cannot believe that the purpose of planning control is to enforce a boring and mediocre uniformity. . . any system of control must make some space for the dynamic, the unexpected and the downright quirky, or we shall all be the poorer for it. I believe that this is one case where a little vision and imagination is appropriate." Whereupon, Mr Power made it clear that he would "try to challenge the decision", a threat that brought from Lord Palumbo, Chairman of the Arts Council, this mild but appallingly true comment: "Most politicians do not know how to lose graciously."

▲ When I am Ruler of the Universe, one of my earliest decrees will lay down that anyone who uses the words "What if everybody did it?" will be fed to Sirius, the Dog Star. It is the last resort of the fun-killers, the oriflamme of the pursed lips brigade, the buttress of those whose motto is "Go and see what Johnny is doing and tell him to stop it". Anyone but a prize nana would have seen that Mr Heine's splendid lark (I pause here to commend the sculptor, Mr John Buckley) was an exact definition of delight, particularly Shakespeare's kind "That give delight and hurt not".

But it hurt the planning committee no end, whence the six years of battle and the preposterous comments (". . . a slap in the face of the decent and respectable people. . .") of its chairman when the battle was finally lost and won.

It is not difficult to see how people get things so devastatingly out of scale; indeed it is one of the most thoroughly studied of human frailties.

I poked fun at the Oxford City Council Planning Committee and in particular its chairman, but that was largely because I had a measure of that body – useful but nothing more. Now suppose you have worked hard and honestly at your job (useful but nothing more), and you dream, or once did dream, of making a mighty stir, of climbing to the heights of being Someone. What

John Power and I in an unusual amicable moment.

is the inevitable knowledge that goes with what has happened to those dreams, and what can be done about it? The knowledge, of course, is that the dreams have not come true; what can be done about it is to exercise that tiny corner of the world in which you do hold sway.

▶ *Man, proud man, dressed in a little brief authority . . . Shakespeare knew humankind, and knew that the briefer the authority the greater the vigour with which it is employed. The Chairman of the Oxford Council Planning Committee does not have the power to have anybody's head cut off, nor to have anybody exiled to Outer Mongolia, nor even to compel anybody to do penance in a white sheet for seven days and seven nights. But he and his council do have the power (exercised, I am sure, only in strict compliance with the law) to order a man with a 25 ft fibreglass shark on his roof to take it off. And when he finds that higher authority has overruled him, he is fit to burst – whence the slap in the face for the decent and respectable people – because even that little authority has been, at least for some time, taken from him.*

Shun power, shun it fiercely, if you want to sleep soundly in your bed. If it is real power, the power to compel others to do your bidding, your dreams will be haunted ones. If it is the mock power of the chairmanship of a municipal committee in Oxford, you will wake to disappointment.

I am not going to quote Acton, but here is Hazlitt, who in this context is even more apposite:

"The love of liberty is the love of others; the love of power is the love of ourselves."

You do not have to be a bad man to want power. Our chairman is plainly an honest and scrupulous man, certainly to be numbered among the decent and respectable people who have figured so largely in this story. But he has forgotten the old and tried proverb: "A man with a stuffed shark on his roof is eccentric, and quite possibly in breach of the planning rules; a man who tries to take the Shark off will run no danger of being bitten, but will almost certainly make a fool of himself.'

The Shark has caught the public imagination, and other journalists get in on the act. The gossip queen of *The Daily Mail*, Lynda Lee-Potter, takes aim at the Shark in an article with a headline that could incite the locals to violence – *Jaws' Neighbours Should Hit the Roof.*

'Bill Heine is the man who has stuck a 25 ft glass-fibre Shark into the roof tiles of his Oxford terrace house. If you're driving quickly past Mr Heine's home you may well think the Shark is droll and amusing.

This, indeed, is the reaction of a Planning Inspector from the Department of the Environment, who has turned down a planning appeal to have it removed, saying:

"I do not believe the purpose of planning control is to enforce a boring and mediocre uniformity."

How imaginative of the inspector, how innovative, how quaintly eccentric – and how safe for him since he lives miles away. I am not giving his precise address, though I'm tempted, because I think Bill Heine's embittered neighbours might go in the dark of night and pitch something large and extremely unboring onto the Inspector's roof.

Certainly if I lived next door to Bill Heine's ugly Shark towering over my garden it would incense me so much I suspect I might scale a ladder armed with an axe, because it's the kind of desperate measure frustrated people resort to when authority kicks them in the teeth.'

What evidence does she have that my neighbours are 'embittered' and why does she think 'authority' has kicked them in the teeth?

Daily Mail columnist – and one of the country's best known – Lynda Lee-Potter comes close to a public apology (after her initial foray attacking supporters of the Shark) with this follow-up article.

A Minister staring into the jaws of defeat

HERITAGE Minister Robert Key is going to try to stop people doing terrible things to the outside of their houses. Good luck to him, I support him wholeheartedly, but he'll have an uphill struggle.

I once wrote a piece sympathising with the neighbours of the man who's got a horrible, 25-foot shark sticking out of his roof. 'They will be pleased with me for supporting them,' I thought smugly.

I was then inundated with furious letters from the shark's neighbours who said they love the ferocious fish, he makes the road seem special, they never want to lose him and in fact every year they have a shark celebration street party.

Several of my neighbours reply, and this letter is typical: 'Well over 90% of the neighbours, far from being embittered, love and take pride in our Shark. If Lynda Lee-Potter likes to visit the Shark, we'll arrange for a ladder and she can see for herself that the Shark is quite harmless, doesn't bite or give off odours – it just likes the view from up there and the people who smile as they go by.'

The reaction is so strong that Lynda Lee-Potter follows up her article with the closest she has ever come to apologising for anything (*see above*). I know people's reactions to the Shark is something that divides them into different camps, and now we have evidence of a new group called 'the smugs'.

The Shark odyssey started with howls of outrage and abuse and it may end with applause and approval. The Headington Shark has been nominated as an Icon of England on a website where voters are asked to rate it with national treasures like Stonehenge, Coronation Street and the original Cowley-built Mini.

An Oxfordshire County Councillor for Headington, Mohammed Altaf-Khan, is prepared to support the iconic status of this former pariah: 'I know that a lot of people now come to Headington just to see the Shark, which has got to be good for the area. It doesn't really disturb the residents living nearby and has now become an important part of the area. I would certainly say it is an iconic piece of work.'

How do I feel about the Shark in my roof as an English Icon? I'm amazed how the English Establishment can reach out and claim the Shark when it has been variously likened to a monstrous carbuncle, a work of art, or just a joke –'whichever way you look at it, the Shark . . . has been one of the most enduring two-fingered gestures ever made to those in authority'.

But there are several Sharks and maybe one of them could be an icon. There is the one that burns itself into people's brains so they take it away with them and live with it for the rest of their lives. This is the Shark that travels well, transcends boundaries and talks to people of different cultures and languages and means millions of different things in each country around the globe.

The Shark is also an adventure and idea that delights and amuses almost everybody and intrigues or puzzles the rest. It is the agile animal that wanders through the committees of Oxford City Council, the corridors of the Crown Court and the offices of Cabinet members, and escapes!

To artist Mark Bridger it is a symbol: 'The councillors, bureaucrats and powers-that-be wanted to crush this expression of artistic originality or eccentricity and a six-year legal battle followed. The Shark, whatever other meanings it may have, represents a significant victory for the freedom of the individual and for artistic expression which for me must make it one of the most important artworks of the late 20th century.'

And then there is the physical art work, gloriously realised by sculptor John Buckley, that still crashes through the tiles of my house. This is the Shark I always return to. And when I'm walking home and see a robin perched on the dorsal fin, silhouetted against the sky and singing its heart out, I still get shivers down my spine after twenty-five years.

And I think back to the beginning on the day this adventure started and one of my neighbours said 'We've got to stop him. If he gets away with this what else will he do?'

That person had a point.

The sculptor John Buckley and I have something else up our sleeves, and if we pull this one off, it will make the Shark look like small fry. ◢

TIMELINE

9 August 1986
Shark nose dives into suburban consciousness

15 October 1986
Oxford City Council Planning Committee refuses permission for the Shark to land

17 November 1986
Full Council confirms Planning Committee refusal

21 November 1986
Shark starts to glow red at night in protest

14 April 1987
Southern Arts Council gives a grant of £1,000 to sculptor John Buckley in recognition of the quality of his previous work and the power of his present work on the Shark

15 July 1987
Planning Committee does a U-turn and approves Shark by a vote of 7–2

27 July 1987
Full Council takes no action and promises further consultation

27 August 1987
Neighbours start 'Jaws Is A Killer' campaign against Shark

17 September 1987
Shark on Oxford City Council Planning meeting agenda

21 October 1987
Planning Committee asks Recreation Committee to find a home for the Shark in a park or pool

26 October 1987
Full Council votes to kill off the Shark at my house but offers alternative site at the Old Fire Station Arts Centre in Oxford or the Temple Cowley Swimming Pool

8 January 1988
Full Council votes to re-site Shark which goes to Planning Committee which passes the ball over to Recreation Committee who lob it back to Planning

7 March 1988
Secret meeting of Planning Committee to demolish Shark if I don't take it down

10 June 1988
Editorial of *Oxford Times* asks how the Shark got airborne

23 March 1989
City Council Chiefs decide to start legal proceedings against me in a secret session

My house 100 years ago – when it had a chimney instead of a Shark.

High Street, New Headington

21 July 1988
Hertford College students in Oxford invite the Shark to crash through their world famous 'Bridge of Sighs' as a new home for the Shark

27 June 1989
I get a summons to appear at the Magistrates Court when I address the full City Council meeting

7 August 1989
I appear at Magistrates' Court and appeal

January 1990
Court case and £1,000 fine

25 January 1990
At Oxford Crown Court case I am fined £1,000 and the Judge orders me to pay £5,000 costs of Oxford City Council's legal bill

26 January 1990
I submit planning application to retain the Shark

4 February 1990
A secret meeting of the Planning Committee decides to rip out the Shark, but they agree first to hear my planning application 'to appear fair'

19 February 1990
Roger Perkins letter is very important here

7 March 1990
Planning Committee considers my application and rejects it

19 March 1990
Mr Great White Shark receives a Poll Tax Bill from Oxford City Council

25 June 1990
Full Council votes 21–20 in favour of keeping the Shark in my roof and sends the application back to the Planning Committee

25 July 1990
Planning Committee approves the Shark

24 September 1990
Full Council disapproves of the Shark

25 October 1990
Planning Committee disagrees with Full Council and approves the Shark

30 October 1990
Full Council votes by majority of 1 to refuse permission for the Shark and sends it back to Planning Committee

14 November 1990
Planning Committee splits evenly 5–5 on the Shark and the Chairman John Power casts his extra tie-breaking vote to kill off the Shark

20, 21 June 1991
Confidential report of Oxford Planning Committee to remove the Shark, but wait for the outcome of a Public Inquiry

15–16 October 1991
Public Inquiry into whether the Shark should stay or go

22 May 1992
Secretary of State for the Environment approves the Shark

2011
Oxford City Council finally acknowledges that the Shark is a work of art by including it on its Public Art Map

THANK YOU

Bill Heine would like to make the following thanks:

to June Whitehouse, Sharkivist of New High Street, without
you would we have a history of this adventure?

to John Simms of Oxford law firm Bower and Bailey, without
you how many court cases would we have?

to Stephanie Jenkins, neighbour and friend, without
you would the Shark have the same bite?

to Editor James Harrison and Designer Nick Withers,
without you would the Shark have landed?

to Simon O'Neil, Editor Oxford Mail and Oxford Times, without
your help this book would have been a long row to hoe.

to Captain Ahab, without you what would Moby Dick be but just another whale?

to Magnus and Jane, without you would there be a book at all?

PICTURE CREDITS AND ACKNOWLEDGMENTS

Oxfordfolio would like to thank the following individuals and organisations for their permission to reproduce photographs and other shark-related ephemera and for their support in the making of this book. We have made every effort to contact the copyright holders for permissions and apologize in advance for any omissions or errors, and we will be pleased to make any necessary changes for future editions.

We are grateful to the *Oxford Mail/Oxford Times* (Newsquest Oxfordshire) for allowing us to use the images on pp.21, 32, 33, 54, 60, 64, 72,73, 122, 128, 130, 141, 144 and especially thanks to Chris McDowell, Librarian, for his efforts in hunting down old clippings; Neil Braggins for scanning the negatives; Jessica Mann, Group Picture Editor, and Mel Costello, Editorial Artist for the map p144; Mark Chamberlain for p.3 pic; Jon Davison p.22, 50; Vivien Shelton, p.116, www.vivienshelton.co.uk; Conrad Hafenrichter conrad @photolives.com for images p.59, 69; Stephen Mayes stephen_mayes@msn.com (p.22); Nur Hussein (Lego® pic) at http://unixcat.org; Colin J Williams Photography aka www.redbubble.com/people/arrowman for his moody Shark (p.36); Matthew Williams for his cool illustration (p.138) and shark colophons, visit his website at www.etch-n-sketch.co.uk; Charles Cutting, (p.139) www.charlescutting.com; Ruth Marsh at *The Daily Telegraph*, Marzanna Mistela at *The Daily Mail*, Ben Smith at *The Times*, the estate of Bernard Levin for permissions to reproduce articles, cuttings and cartoons; John Mair and his wife Susan for encouragement and advice; Keith Barnes at Photographers Workshop, Oxford, www.oxofordschool of photography.co.uk for the scans; Stephanie Jenkins of www.headington.org.uk for all her behind the scenes input, the image p.140, and not least proof reading and copy editing. Silhouette on page 1© Winning Moves UK Ltd 2011, ©1935, 2008 Hasbro. All rights reserved.

If you want to nominate the Shark as your 'Icon of England' visit *www.icons.org.uk*

VISIT WWW.OXFORDFOLIO.CO.UK

ABOUT THE AUTHOR

Although Bill Heine is not English, he still likes them. This attraction
grew while Bill was a lifeguard at Batavia Quarry Pool in Illinois.
He thought it would be more fun saving lives in Oxford.

After swimming, Bill went to Washington DC, studied at Georgetown University and
worked in the United States Senate and the Executive Office of the White House.

Balliol College in Oxford invited him to read law. Bill thought he needed to know
how a society was held together if he wanted to take it apart. Bill stayed in Oxford
ever since and grew so fond of the place he decided to give it a gift of a Shark.

The rest is . . . a disaster

HOW TO FIND THE SHARK